The Holocaust: Death Camps

Tamara L. Roleff, *Book Editor*

Daniel Leone, *Publisher*
Bonnie Szumski, *Editorial Director*
Scott Barbour, *Managing Editor*
David M. Haugen, *Series Editor*

Greenhaven Press, Inc., San Diego, California

Every effort has been made to trace the owners of copyrighted material. The articles in this volume may have been edited for content, length, and/or reading level. The titles have been changed to enhance the editorial purpose.

No part of this book may be reproduced or used in any form or by any means, electrical, mechanical, or otherwise, including, but not limited to, photocopy, recording, or any information storage and retrieval system, without prior permission from the publisher.

Library of Congress Cataloging-in-Publication Data

The Holocaust: death camps / Tamara L. Roleff.
   p.   cm. — (History firsthand)
  Includes bibliographical references (p.   ) and index.
  ISBN 0-7377-0882-4 (pbk. : alk. paper)
  ISBN 0-7377-0883-2 (lib. : alk. paper)
  1. Holocaust, Jewish (1939–1945)—Personal narratives. 2. Jews—Persecutions—Europe. 3. World War, 1939–1945—Concentration camps. I. Roleff, Tamara L., 1959– II. Series.

D804.3 .H639 2002
940.53'18—dc21   2001033208

Printed in the USA

Contents

Chapter 1: Arrival

1. The Train Ride to Auschwitz
by Rena Kornreich Gelissen   37
Jews who obeyed the Nazi summons for deportation to "work camps" endured almost unbearable misery on the train ride to the concentration camps. Forced into cattle cars, the inmates had only the food and drink they brought with them, which often proved to be inadequate for their journey. Toilet facilities were nonexistent, and the stench soon became unbearable. Many people died during the trip.

2. Old and Sick to the Left, Healthy to the Right
by Leo Fettman   42
All trains arriving at the camps were met by high-ranking camp officials, who made the first of many "selections." Men and women were separated into groups and quickly examined by the Nazis. The old, the very young, pregnant women, and the ill were motioned to the left, and subsequently to their death, while the healthy and strong were sent to the right, to be kept alive to work, at least for a while.

3. The First Day
by Sara Tuvel Bernstein   49
After surviving the first selection, the new inmates were completely shaven and given rags for clothes. What followed would be a typical day in the camp; the prisoners were fed a thin soup and forced to sleep on wooden bunks with no blankets. While standing for hours the next morning during roll call, the inmates watched as guards entered the barracks and carried out bodies of women who had been alive the night before.

Chapter 2: Work Detail

1. The Intellectual as Laborer

Inmates who were skilled craftsmen and laborers fared better in the concentration camps than businessmen or professionals. The Nazis frequently made intellectuals perform hard labor, which was usually a death sentence for those who did not have much bodily strength. Intellectuals also had trouble adjusting to the rough life in the camps, and their ostracism by working-class inmates left them isolated and often contributed to their early deaths.

2. The Special Work Detail

The *sonderkommando* was a special work detail that included handling the dead bodies that were ready for the crematorium. The workers shaved the bodies, searched them for gold, diamonds, and other valuables, and transferred the corpses from the gas chambers to the crematoriums.

3. A Nurse at Auschwitz

Hospitals in the concentration camps were extremely primitive. Medical supplies, equipment, medicine, and trained personnel were rarely available. Nevertheless, those who worked in the hospitals and infirmaries tried their best to ease the suffering of their fellow inmates.

Chapter 3: Survival and Daily Life

1. Roll Call

Roll call was an integral part of life in the concentration camp. It was used not only to count the prisoners several times a day, but also as a form of punishment and torture for the inmates, as they were forced to stand for hours in any type of weather.

Chapter 4: Confronting Death

second who would die and who would live for a while longer. The selection process could be influenced by an inmate's sickly appearance, but sometimes it was simply a matter of the officers' whim.

Chapter 5: The Germans

so would cause subordinate SS officers and extermination camp guards to doubt the righteousness of the Nazi cause.

Chapter 6: Liberation

Foreword

In his preface to a book on the events leading to the Civil War, Stephen B. Oates, the historian and biographer of Abraham Lincoln, John Brown, and other noteworthy American historical figures, explained the difficulty of writing history in the traditional third-person voice of the biographer and historian. "The trouble, I realized, was the detached third-person voice," wrote Oates. "It seemed to wring all the life out of my characters and the antebellum era." Indeed, how can a historian, even one as prominent as Oates, compete with the eloquent voices of Daniel Webster, Abraham Lincoln, Harriet Beecher Stowe, Frederick Douglass, and Robert E. Lee?

Oates's comment notwithstanding, every student of history, professional and amateur alike, can name a score of excellent accounts written in the traditional third-person voice of the historian that bring to life an event or an era and the people who lived through it. In *Battle Cry of Freedom*, James M. McPherson vividly re-creates the American Civil War. Barbara Tuchman's *The Guns of August* captures in sharp detail the tensions in Europe that led to the outbreak of World War I. Taylor Branch's *Parting the Waters* provides a detailed and dramatic account of the American Civil Rights Movement. The study of history would be impossible without such guiding texts.

Nonetheless, Oates's comment makes a compelling point. Often the most convincing tellers of history are those who lived through the event, the eyewitnesses who recorded their firsthand experiences in autobiographies, speeches, memoirs, journals, and letters. The Greenhaven Press History Firsthand series presents history through the words of first-person narrators. Each text in this series captures a significant historical era or event—the American Civil War, the

Great Depression, the Holocaust, the Roaring Twenties, the 1960s, the Vietnam War. Readers will investigate these historical eras and events by examining primary-source documents, authored by chroniclers both famous and little known. The texts in the History Firsthand series comprise the celebrated and familiar words of the presidents, generals, and famous men and women of letters who recorded their impressions for posterity, as well as the statements of the ordinary people who struggled to understand the storm of events around them—the foot soldiers who fought the great battles and their loved ones back home, the men and women who waited on the breadlines, the college students who marched in protest.

The texts in this series are particularly suited to students beginning serious historical study. By examining these firsthand documents, novice historians can begin to form their own insights and conclusions about the historical era or event under investigation. To aid the student in that process, the texts in the History Firsthand series include introductions that provide an overview of the era or event, timelines, and bibliographies that point the serious student toward key historical works for further study.

The study of history commences with an examination of words—the testimony of witnesses who lived through an era or event and left for future generations the task of making sense of their accounts. The Greenhaven Press History Firsthand series invites the beginner historian to commence the process of historical investigation by focusing on the words of those individuals who made history by living through it and recording their experiences firsthand.

Introduction

The Nazi Death Camps

L ong before Adolf Hitler rose to power in Germany, he was fanatical in his hatred of the Jews. His anti-Semitism was revealed early in his life in his half-autobiographical and half-ideological treatise *Mein Kampf (My Struggle)*. In *Mein Kampf*, written nearly a decade before he was named chancellor of Germany in 1933, Hitler refers to Jews as "maggots,"[1] "a pestilence,"[2] "parasites,"[3] a "vampire"[4] and "the personification of the devil as the symbol of all evil."[5] Hitler believed that Jews were deliberately trying to defile and contaminate the racial purity of the Aryans (non-Jewish Caucasians), who he believed were superior in all respects to every other race. According to Hitler and his followers, the Germans were at the top of the racial pyramid; below them ranked other Aryan nationalities, followed by Poles, Czechs, and other Slavs, Gypsies, and blacks. At the bottom of the list were the Jews.

Hitler's racism and anti-Semitism became the central tenet of his Nazi Party's ideology and was the driving force behind German conduct and policy during World War II. In fact, Hitler saw himself as the world's savior, ridding the world of Jews and other subhumans. Once the Jews were exterminated, Hitler believed the world would no longer suffer from wars, famines, economic depressions, and other misfortunes and tragedies. The dilemma was how to solve the Jewish "problem" or "question."

Hitler gave early hints of the annihilation he planned for the Jews. In *Mein Kampf*, he argued that the deaths of mil-

11

lions of German soldiers during World War I would have been worth it if Jews had also died:

> If at the beginning of the War and during the War twelve or fifteen thousand of the Hebrew corrupters of the people had been held under poison gas, as happened to hundreds of thousands of our very best German workers in the field, the sacrifice of millions at the front would not have been in vain.[6]

Hitler's desire for the extermination of the Jews and others he felt were undesirable was one that he would pursue the rest of his life.

In March 1933, through some political maneuvering, Hitler became the Führer, Germany's leader, or more accurately, dictator. He did not wait long to begin persecuting the Jews. In April 1933, the Nazi-controlled Reichstag (parliament) passed laws that severely restricted the Jews' economic, educational, and personal freedoms. Every year new restrictions were passed against the Jews. In April 1938, Jews who had not fled from Hilter's tyranny were forcibly moved from their villages and towns into walled-off sections of larger cities called ghettos. This grouping together of large numbers of Jews made it much easier for the Germans to later round up and transport them to the concentration camps, thus dooming millions of Jews to their deaths.

In a speech in January 1939, just nine months before he invaded Poland, setting off World War II, Hitler simultaneously blamed the Jews for his future actions and warned the world about his intentions for them: "Today I will once more be a prophet: if they [the Jews] succeed in plunging the nations once more into a world war, then the result [will be] the annihilation of the Jewish race in Europe."[7] Most did not take Hitler's threat to exterminate all the European Jews seriously; at the time, only four hundred thousand Jews were under the control of the Nazis. However, as Hitler began his campaign of expanding the Third Reich, the number of Jews under German domination increased exponentially. Germany's occupation of Poland brought more than

3 million Jews under Hitler's power. After the crushing defeat of Poland, the Nazis ordered that Jews publicly identify themselves. In most countries, this identification consisted of a yellow six-pointed star that was sewn onto their clothing; in other countries, Jews were forced to wear a white band with a blue Star of David on it.

Operation T-4

The answer to Germany's "Jewish question" began to emerge when Hitler authorized a program to keep the new "master race" strong and pure by eliminating those the Führer considered *Lebens unwertes Leben* (life unworthy of life). Physically and mentally handicapped children were the first subjects to be systematically killed in the euthanasia program known as Operation T-4. Later, the elderly, incurably ill, mentally ill, and emotionally disturbed were added to the list of acceptable victims. Those who were selected to die were transported to one of six killing centers, where they were either starved to death, given a lethal injection, or gassed in a room disguised as a shower. Afterward, gold teeth were extracted from their mouths and the bodies were cremated. The ashes were returned to their families with a note that said the patient had died a natural death.

Protests against the euthanasia program by religious leaders forced Operation T-4 to be officially discontinued in August 1941; however, it quietly continued underground until the end of the war. It is estimated that between seventy and eighty thousand people were killed between 1939 and 1945 in the T-4 program.

The *Einsatzgruppen*

Operation T-4 was the model for the extermination camps to come, but it was not the only method the Germans used for killing those deemed unworthy of life. Following the German invasion of the Soviet Union in June 1941, the *Wehrmacht* (German army) brought in four special action squads called *Einsatzgruppen* to round up Jews and other "undesirables." The *Einsatzgruppen* were made up of German police, SS officers, and local residents who volunteered for the job. These special action squads made the policy of state-sponsored genocide official. The *Einsatzgruppen* followed behind the army, rounding up all the Jews, Gypsies, Communists, and intelligentsia in the area, and then marching them to an isolated field or forest. The *Einsatzgruppen* then shot all the victims with machine guns and rifles. Using the *Einsatzgruppen,* the Nazis systematically murdered more than 1 million Communists and Jews one by one in the Soviet Union and Poland.

Although most of the three thousand men involved in the *Einsatzgruppen* seemed to enjoy their work, laughing and joking about the Jews they were killing, the continual screams from the victims, and the blood, gore, and splattered brains began to have an effect on the soldiers. One Nazi officer complained that the *Einsatzgruppen*

> firing squads could not cope with the psychological and moral stress of the mass shootings indefinitely. I know that a number of members of these squads were themselves committed to mental asylums and for this reason a new and better method of killing [has] to be found.[8]

The "new and better method of killing" was the development of mobile gas vans and gas chambers in the concentration camps.

The Final Solution

The Nazis had been sending Jews, Communists, political prisoners, Gypsies, homosexuals, Jehovah's Witnesses, Freemasons, and, after the invasion of the Soviet Union, prisoners of war to concentration camps since shortly after Hitler took power in 1933. Dachau, a concentration camp in southern Germany, was the first to open in March 1933. By the end of the war in May 1945, the Nazis had established more than nine thousand camps in Germany and German-occupied territories. The camps included transit camps, labor camps, detention camps, and prisoner-of-war camps. There were even camps for children whose parents were working in labor camps and more than three hundred camps for women only.

Hitler's top aides met in January 1942 to discuss the "Final Solution" to the "Jewish question." According to Adolf Eichmann, head of the Gestapo office dealing with Jewish affairs, the fifteen men at the conference "spoke about methods of killing, about liquidation, about extermination [of the Jews]."[9] Although the policy of Jewish genocide was now finalized, the fact is that the Germans had begun testing the technology needed for the mass murder of the Jews several months before. Rudolf Höss, commandant of the Auschwitz camp, had experimented with Zyklon-B, a poison made of hydrogen cyanide, in September 1941. In this experiment, about 850 people, 600 of whom were Soviet prisoners of war, were killed with the deadly gas in a small chamber in the camp. The concentration camp at Chelmno began gassing prisoners on a regular basis as of December 8, 1941, a day after Pearl Harbor was bombed by the Japanese.

Now that the Nazis had finalized the Final Solution to the Jewish problem, the SS could concentrate on sending European Jews to their deaths in the concentration camps instead of having the *Einsatzgruppen* kill them. Six camps— all in Poland—were designated as extermination centers for Jews and other "undesirables." The camps—Chelmno, Belzec, Sobibor, Treblinka, Majdanek, and Auschwitz— were all located on a main railroad in Poland for several reasons: Poland, after the Soviet Union, had the largest concentration of Jews—well over 3 million—in Europe. Poland also had a long history of anti-Semitism that would prove useful to German efforts to eradicate the Jews. Finally, the camps could not be located in Germany, where protests from church leaders and Germans could derail the execution of the plan, as had happened to Operation T-4.

The Death Camps

Chelmno, in northern Poland, was the first death camp where Jews were killed in the gas vans on a regular basis. By September 1942, fifty-five thousand adult Jews, twenty thousand Jewish children, and five thousand Gypsies from the Lodz ghetto had been sent to the gas vans in Chelmno. Here the Nazis used vans disguised as Red Cross vehicles—each of which could hold up to seventy people—to kill people with carbon monoxide gas. A witness to the killings at Chelmno describes what it was like:

> The back door of the van would be open. The Jews were made to get inside the van. This job was done by three Poles, who I believe were sentenced to death. The Poles hit the Jews with whips if they did not get in the gas-vans fast enough. . . . The driver then switched on the engine, crawled under the van and connected a pipe from the exhaust to the inside of the van. The exhaust fumes now poured into the inside of the truck so that the people inside were suffocated. After about ten minutes, when there were no further signs of life from the Jews, the van set off toward the camp in the woods where the bodies were then burned.[10]

Chelmno was the only death camp that used vans to gas its victims. By the time the Russian army liberated Chelmno in January 1945, more than 150,000 Jews, Poles, Gypsies, and Soviet POWs had been murdered there.

Permanent gas chambers were built in the remaining death camps to kill Jews and those deemed unworthy of life. The chambers could accommodate much larger numbers of victims than the vans could, and they needed far fewer SS and army officers to oversee the killings. Three death camps—Belzec, Sobibor, and Treblinka—all became operational within a few months of each other in 1942.

One of Belzec's gas chambers was a chamber that had been used in the T-4 euthanasia program; it had been dismantled and shipped to Belzec, where it was reassembled. The gas chambers at Sobibor and Treblinka also used carbon monoxide to kill the Jews who were shipped there. The rooms were similar to those at Belzec—about thirteen feet by twenty-six feet with low ceilings. Exhaust fumes from an engine installed in a shed near the gas chamber were piped into the room. In just over a year, the Nazis murdered between 550,000 and 600,000 people—mostly Jews—at Belzec; 200,000 to 250,000 Jews at Sobibor; and between 750,000 and 870,000 at Treblinka. Nearly all of these people were dead within a few hours of their arrival at the camps.

The poison Zyklon-B was used in the gas chambers at Majdanek and Auschwitz. Before Majdanek was liberated

Major Concentration Camps in Europe, 1938–1945

○ Large-scale labor camps
■ Large-scale extermination camps

in July 1944, about 50,000 prisoners had been gassed there. Another 360,000 died from starvation, disease, beatings, and exhaustion.

Auschwitz is perhaps the most notorious of the Holocaust concentration camps, although at the time very few people had ever heard of it. Auschwitz was actually three separate camps: Auschwitz I (a concentration camp); Auschwitz II (also known as Birkenau or Auschwitz-Birkenau, the extermination camp); and Auschwitz III (or Auschwitz-Monowitz or Buna-Monowitz, a slave-labor camp). Auschwitz-Birkenau was the most efficient of the six extermination camps. Höss, the camp's commandant from May 1940 until December 1943, boasted that each of his four gas chambers could kill 2,000 people at a time. It is believed that about 1.5 million Jews were murdered there. Also killed at Auschwitz were approximately 19,000 Gypsies and 12,000 Soviet POWs. Another 500,000 died from other causes.

The Execution of the Final Solution

Most of those who were sent to the concentration camps arrived via freight trains. Each boxcar would be packed with eighty to one hundred people or more for a journey that might last a week. Some cars were so crowded that the travelers had no room to sit or lie down. A bucket in a corner served as the toilet. The only food to eat and water to drink was what the prisoners brought themselves. People frequently died in the summer from the heat and in the winter from the cold. The passengers were forced to keep the corpses with them until they arrived at their destination, because the Germans locked the boxcar doors from the outside. Joseph Tyl, a Catholic priest, was working at the station in a death camp when a new trainload of French internees arrived. He recounts the horror of what he witnessed:

> The Nazi monsters had squeezed 100 to 140 people into each boxcar. I remember in my own case, where there were only fifty to a

car, that we still could neither breathe nor move, and I wondered how people could survive under these circumstances. The people I now saw arriving had all died of asphyxiation. Their faces had turned black, and their lips were horribly swollen. There were several truckloads of corpses in this condition.[11]

Most of the travelers had no idea of their fate. Although they may have heard rumors in the ghetto of death camps, most Jews refused to believe them. The Germans did everything they could to keep up the fiction that the Jews were merely being moved to new settlements in the east or to labor camps where they could work. They encouraged the Jews to bring their clothing and valuables with them. In addition, the train stations in the camps were made to look like ordinary train stations. Auschwitz's arrival platform had train schedules posted and flowers and shrubs planted, and the camp band played show tunes.

Shattered Hopes

Any hopes the newly arrived prisoners may have held about their future were soon shattered. When the doors to the boxcars were opened, they were greeted with shouts and beatings from the guards. The prisoners were ordered to leave all their luggage behind on the platform. The guards then told their charges they were going to take a shower. The new arrivals were lulled into a false sense of security by signs along the way to the gas chamber that read, in various languages, "To the baths." The charade continued when the prisoners reached the waiting room, which adjoined the gas chamber. There the guards ordered the prisoners to hand over all their jewelry. Then everyone—men, women, and children—was instructed to strip in preparation for their shower. Usually the prisoners were hesitant about undressing in front of each other until the guards started beating them. One witness recalls that the Nazis continued the deception of a shower, even up to the moment the prisoners entered the chamber:

The new arrivals who were to be gassed undressed in the waiting room. This room was a model of Hitlerian hypocrisy and lies. It was luxuriously appointed, and there were clothes hangers along the walls with enameled plates above them that bore the following message in various languages: "If you want to find your clothes again as you leave, be sure to remember your [clothes hanger] number."[12]

Death in the Gas Chambers

Next, the guards drove the naked prisoners into the gas chambers. The victims were packed tightly into a room, usually so closely that each victim only had about one square foot of space in which to stand. After all the prisoners were inside, the guards locked the doors from the outside, and the gassing began. Death usually resulted in just a few minutes for those exposed to Zyklon-B and about thirty minutes for those faced with carbon monoxide gas.

After all the prisoners had died, the doors to the gas chambers were opened and a special work detail of prisoners started pulling out the corpses. It was not an easy job; during the gassing, the people inside the chamber had panicked and tried to find some way to escape. Filip Müller, a Czech Jew who was assigned to work in the crematorium at Auschwitz, was horrified by what he saw. The victims had struggled to survive by pushing and climbing on top of each other in an effort to reach clean air near the ceiling. During their fight for life, children, women, and the weak ended up at the bottom of the pile of bodies. When the gas chamber doors were opened,

> The people were battered. They struggled and fought in the darkness. They were covered in excrement, in blood, from ears and noses. One sometimes saw that the people lying on the ground, because of the pressure of the others, were unrecognizable. Children had their skulls crushed. It was awful. Vomit. Blood—from the ears and noses, probably even menstrual fluid. I'm sure of it. There was everything in that struggle for life, that death struggle. It was terrible to see.[13]

Müller's job, and that of others who were assigned to the special work detail in the camps, was to shave the corpses (their hair was then disinfected and used in making felt and stuffing furniture), search the bodies for hidden valuables, and remove gold teeth. Then Müller and the other workers hauled the dead bodies to the crematoriums or pits outside, where they would be burned. The special work detail workers had a short life expectancy in the death camps; the Nazis killed everyone in the work details every few months in an attempt to keep the Final Solution a secret from the outside world. Müller escaped before the Nazis could kill him.

Not All Are Gassed

Not all prisoners were sent immediately to the gas chambers. All the camps needed prisoners for labor of some kind, if only to sort through the gassed victims' belongings or carry the corpses to the crematoriums or pits to be burned. Prisoners were also used to build or enlarge the concentration and extermination camps. Auschwitz and Majdanek also had labor camps, so some new arrivals were spared to work in nearby factories or in the fields to produce food for the inmates and guards.

When the labor or extermination camps needed workers, the new arrivals went through an immediate "selection." This procedure determined whether a person would be sent to the gas chamber or chosen to work. As soon as the doors to the boxcars were opened, the new arrivals were sorted into two lines—one for women and children, the other for men and boys. High-ranking Nazi officers then made a cursory inspection of all the arrivals, sending mothers with their young children, the elderly, and the sick and weak to the left side of the platform. These people were selected for the gas chambers. The Nazis calmed these prisoners' fears by telling them they were being taken to the hospital or would be given lighter work assignments. Sometimes, healthy prisoners would ask the guards for permission to join family members who had been sent to the left, not realizing they were asking to be sent to their death. Permission was readily granted. Other times, prisoners would try to warn the new arrivals to lie about their age. Mothers were told to say their children were older than they were, while older adults were advised to say they were younger than they were. Clara L. tells how the workers helped save some young women from the gas chambers at Auschwitz:

> They would say to these young women who carried their babies on their arms, "Give it to your mother, give it to your mother-in-law. Don't be a fool! You can save your life." And many, many women did that. They handed their babies to the older women and they went to the working side and they were saved. Their children perished.[14]

The new arrivals who survived the initial selection were marched to an area of the camp where they were forced to strip, had their hair shaved, and were disinfected. After a brief cold shower, they had to wait outside—in any kind of weather—to receive their clothing, which was generally inadequate and ill fitting. Usually, but not always, they were then tattooed with a number. According to Anita Lasker-Wallfisch, every step in the process was designed to dehumanize the prisoners and undermine their will to resist:

> The tattooing was not a pleasant experience, especially if you bear in mind how primitive the tool with which it was carried out was. It looked something like a penholder except that instead of a nib it had a thick needle at the end. Of course it hurt. There was blood and a nasty swelling afterwards. Very likely it became infected. I don't believe for one moment that this tattooing tool was ever disinfected. I suppose I should regard myself as fortunate in that the girl who tattooed me had reasonably neat handwriting. The numbers that now adorn my left forearm are not outsize and all over the place like some I have seen. Maybe the shaving off of my hair was in fact the most traumatic experience. It made me feel totally naked, utterly vulnerable and reduced to a complete *nobody*. By now I had relinquished my clothes as well, and I stood there stark naked, without any hair and with a number on my arm. In the space

of a few minutes I had been stripped of every vestige of human dignity and become indistinguishable from everyone around me.[15]

The Barracks

After the prisoners were shaved, disinfected, tattooed, and issued clothing, they were assigned to a barracks. The barracks were generally wooden buildings with no insulation, one central door, and few, if any, windows. Some barracks had originally been built as stables. The inmates slept on wooden bunks that had been built in three tiers. Depending on the size of the bunk, ten to twenty people were forced to share space that might have sufficed for two or four. Some bunks had straw mattresses, many did not. Pillows were nonexistent, and one blanket per bunk was the norm. The inmates were purposely overcrowded; a single barracks might contain eight hundred or a thousand adults.

The prisoners also shared their barracks with lice and bed bugs. With no opportunity to wash their bodies, their clothes, or their bedding, there was little the victims could do to protect themselves from becoming infested. Besides suffering from incessant bites, which the inmates scratched until they bled, the prisoners were threatened by disease—especially typhus—which was transmitted by lice.

Food

The barracks were not just for sleeping. The inmates spent what little free time they had there resting or eating. The inmates were consumed by the thought of food. The new arrivals in the barracks—who may have had nothing to eat or drink for several days prior to their arrival—often had to wait one or two days more before they received any food. Food was strictly rationed by the guards, and it usually took some time before the arrival of new prisoners was duly recorded in the kitchen's log. Many new arrivals found it difficult at first to eat the food they received. They willingly gave it away to inmates who had been there longer and therefore were used to eating food that would be considered

inedible under other circumstances. Later, starving but desperate inmates would trade their treasured bowl of watery
soup or sawdust bread with well-connected prisoners for necessities such as shoes, better clothing, or medicine. Olga
Lengyel, who worked as a nurse in Auschwitz, gave up her
ration of bread for eight days for a piece of cloth to make a
blouse, and then she paid three soups to have it sewn.
"Whether to feed or clothe oneself was the eternal problem
facing us,"[16] she notes.

The Black Market

Resourceful inmates could find everything they needed in
the camps to survive. The key was "organizing"—prisoner
slang for scrounging, trading, or stealing—what was
needed. Even the Nazis recognized the necessity of organizing in the camps. Höss, the commandant at Auschwitz,
is said to have declared that anyone who did not resort to
organizing would not last six months in Auschwitz.

Despite being in a closed environment where every piece
of personal property was immediately taken from the prisoners, it was not too difficult for inmates to obtain new clothing, fresh fruit, or even liquor if they had something suitable
to trade or were willing to give up their food ration. The key
to organizing was "Canada," the warehouses where the belongings of the new arrivals were sorted, so known because
Canada was thought to be a wealthy country. The Canada
work detail was highly coveted by the prisoners because the
workers were well fed. They were permitted to eat any food
they found in the luggage, but they were not allowed to take
anything out of the warehouse. Even though the workers
faced severe punishment or even death for bringing items
from Canada back into the camp, many still managed to
smuggle in food, money, jewels, clothing, cigarettes, liquor,
and other valuable contraband, which they would then give
as presents to their friends or trade for other necessities. "The
acquisitions of the Canada detachment were a valuable addition to camp life, even if this was not immediately appar-

ent on an individual basis," explains Lucie Adelsberger, a doctor at Auschwitz. "All of our few possessions, every comb and every toothbrush, came from this source. Effective medications could be gotten nowhere else."[17] However, to be caught with any form of contraband—food, money, or cigarettes, for example—was to risk death from the guards. Yet to go without meant death as well.

Work Details

There were other highly desirable work details, or *kommandos*, in the camps other than in Canada. Jobs in the kitchen were in great demand because the workers could usually find a way to get extra food for themselves and their family and friends. Those who worked in the "sauna," as the gas chamber's undressing room was known, had their choice of the clothing left by the new arrivals. Doctors, nurses, and orderlies sometimes had better food and more privacy than the inmates they tended, but not always.

Most inmates, however, were not lucky enough to work in a *kommando* where they could be assured of getting enough to eat. The Nazi goal was to literally work the inmates—both men and women—to death. Any lifting or carrying of heavy objects was always performed at a run. For many prisoners, such as Octave Rabaté, much of their work was useless, designed simply to exhaust the prisoners. "[My work] consisted of lugging heavy stones from one end of the quarry to the other and from the bottom to the top and then back again—always in double time."[18] Women were not immune from working in hard labor details. Jacqueline Hereil recalls that some of the women in her camp "chopped wood, felled trees, unloaded ships, built roads, drained swamps, pulled rollers. I myself, together with nineteen comrades, pulled a roller."[19] The prisoners were forced to work twelve or fourteen hours a day, with only a half-hour break for lunch, six days a week. The pace was exhausting.

Work was no easier in the factories, where the prisoners worked as slave laborers for prominent German corporations such as Krupps and BMW. According to Hereil, "All the women who did men's work, as well as those who did women's work—like, for example, weaving—were pushed so hard to work at peak performance that they were not allowed to raise their heads from their work for even one second."[20] When prisoners were caught resting, even for just a second, the guards would punish them with a few lashes with a whip, beatings with a club, or some exhausting physical exercise until they dropped dead of exhaustion. Frequently the guards would beat or kill the prisoners simply for their own amusement. A report made after the war concerning the treatment of prisoners at Auschwitz-Birkenau noted that, if an SS officer guarding prisoners at a nearby gravel pit thought one of the workers was "dragging his feet," the guard would wait until the prisoner was climbing up out of the pit and then "simply give him a push and watch him slide with his loaded wheelbarrow all the way back down the slope. For the guards this was a favorite way of passing the time."[21]

Selections

The camp prisoners—whether they were Jewish, Polish, prisoners of war, homosexuals, or political prisoners—had to face the possibility of dying every day from starvation, disease, exhaustion, beatings, and overwork. But Jewish inmates faced another threat—the selections. Despite having passed the initial selection and being allowed to work, the Nazis scheduled additional selections on a regular basis to reduce the camp population when a new shipment of prisoners was expected. Only the strongest and healthiest were permitted to live for a while longer.

The very word *selection* struck fear in the inmates' hearts; they knew they were being sent to the gas chambers. No one knew, however, why the selection officers chose one prisoner over another; it could be because one had a bruise, or a pimple, or a slight limp, or an open sore. Both men and women were forced to run naked in front of the guards during a selection, so it was impossible to conceal any weakness or deformity. Sometimes the selected inmates would be led to the gas chambers immediately; sometimes they would have a few more days until they were led to their deaths. Most Jewish prisoners would not leave the camps alive, and they knew it.

Escapes

A few prisoners were lucky and managed to escape from the camps, but such instances were extremely rare. Those who managed to escape were usually caught by the SS guards, returned to the camp, and executed in front of all the prisoners. The prisoners in the camp were always severely punished after an escape attempt. The Nazis might execute everyone in the escapee's barracks or pull out every tenth prisoner during roll call and shoot them. This fear of retribution led many inmates to foil the escape attempts of their fellow prisoners.

There were a few instances in which mass escapes were successful. In these cases, the prisoners organized and planned a revolt against their guards: at Treblinka on August 2, 1943; at Sobibor on October 14, 1943; and at Auschwitz-Birkenau on October 7, 1944. These three revolts followed a similar pattern. By the summer of 1943, shipments of prisoners to the death camps were slowing; most of the Polish Jews had been exterminated. Prisoners working as *sonderkommando*—special work details in the crematoriums—knew that with no work, the Germans would soon send them to the gas chambers. So the workers in the *sonderkommandos* either stole weapons from the arsenals in the camp or managed to have them smuggled into the camp by resistance fighters on the outside. Then, a signal was given and the inmates started killing as many guards as possible. At the same time, other inmates set fire to the camp or, in the case of Auschwitz, blew up one of the crematoriums. During the confusion, the prisoners—those involved in the planning as well as those who were not—fled the camps.

In all the cases, the number of prisoners who were killed or recaptured during the escape attempts was far higher than the number of those who escaped and were never recaptured. Of the 350 to 400 prisoners who escaped at Treblinka, about 100 eluded recapture or execution. Half of the 600 prisoners in Sobibor escaped, although only 100 or so survived the war. The harsh Polish winter and the local population—who believed the prisoners were carrying gold—killed the rest. A year later at Auschwitz-Birkenau, half of the 600 prisoners who escaped were recaptured and executed.

The Closing of the Camps

By 1943, most of the 3 million Polish Jews had been exterminated. Heinrich Himmler, the commander of the SS and the overseer of the concentration camps in eastern Poland, decided to close Belzec, Sobibor, and Treblinka. The remaining Jews in Eastern Europe, he decided, could be shipped to Auschwitz. The prisoners remaining in the camps were either killed or shipped to another camp. Belzec was the first camp to be closed in July 1943. The Germans dismantled Treblinka in November 1943 and Sobibor in December.

Majdanek

The Allied advance on German-occupied territory in 1944 and 1945—the Soviet armies from the east, the British and Americans from the west—forced the Germans to abandon and evacuate the remaining death camps. The Nazis did not want to leave any witnesses behind who could testify about the atrocities in the camps. Because workers were still needed for the German war effort, the prisoners were moved to camps in central Germany instead of simply killed where they were. However, the Germans ran out of time at Majdanek. Although they had started evacuating prisoners in March, there were still approximately a thousand prisoners left when the Russians liberated the death camp on July 23, 1944. The Russians were horrified by what they found in the camp—starving and emaciated prisoners, gas chambers, crematoriums, bodies of prisoners who had not yet been cremated rotting in the sun, and about 800,000 pairs of shoes.

The Russians invited the International Red Cross and the news media to Majdanek to see the horror for themselves. In October, the *Illustrated London News* published twelve photographs taken in the camp. It apologized in advance for publishing photos of the atrocities,

> but in view of the fact the enormity of the crimes perpetrated by the Germans is so wicked that our readers, to whom such behavior is unbelievable, may think the reports of such crimes exaggerated or due to propaganda, we consider it necessary to present them, by means of the accompanying photographs, with irrefutable proof of the organized murder of between 600,000 and 1,000,000 helpless persons at the Majdanek Camp near Lublin. And even these pictures are carefully selected from a number, some of which are too horrible to reproduce. . . .
>
> The story as it stands is almost incredible in its bestiality, but German cruelty went further still at Majdanek. Prisoners too ill to walk into the camp . . . were dragged alive to the furnaces and thrust in alongside the dead.[22]

Despite the best efforts of the Soviets and the Red Cross, the photos and stories coming from Majdanek were dismissed as exaggerations and propaganda by both Hitler and most of the world.

The Nazis who worked in the death camps, however, knew that the photos and stories from Majdanek were not exaggerations. When the Soviets closed in on Auschwitz in January 1945, the Nazis made a valiant attempt to obliterate all evidence of what had occurred there. They blew up the crematoriums, burned all the records, and destroyed most of the warehouses storing goods stolen from the prisoners. The notorious Nazi physician Joseph Mengele fled to Berlin with the records of his gruesome experiments at the camps. During the last roll call in Auschwitz on January 17, 1945, the Nazis counted 67,012 prisoners. The next day the Nazis began their death marches to other concentration camps in central Germany. A quarter of these prisoners died during their forced marches.

The Death Marches

The death march from Auschwitz is typical of the fifty-nine death marches from Nazi concentration camps conducted in the winter and spring of 1944–1945. The prisoners were marched for days with little food, water, or rest. Anyone who could not keep up was shot. Some groups of prisoners were marched to railway stations, where they then rode freight trains to their destination; others were forced to go on foot for the entire distance, sometimes for hundreds of miles. Both methods were difficult. According to Paul Kuziner, the train ride out of the camp was just as bad as their original ride to the camp. The Germans "crammed us into coal cars without a roof, 140 people per car. We remained in these cars for three days and three nights, standing, squeezed against each other, unable to sit or sleep."[23]

Michel Scheckter had to march on very little food for "fifty-two days straight. For food we got three to five potatoes. Ten times during this march we got soup and a quarter-liter of wine, and four times we got margarine."[24] They were marched on back roads so that the main routes would be free for military vehicles. It was difficult to take care of bodily functions during the march. "Those who needed to relieve themselves had to run ahead of the group, squat by the side of the road, and be dressed again by the time the rest of the group caught up with them; otherwise they would be shot on the spot."[25]

Because of the bitter cold, the lack of food, the poor physical condition of the marchers, and the general ruthlessness of the guards, the death rates during the marches were astounding, ranging from a low of 25 percent to 90 percent or even higher. Scheckter notes that, of the three hundred prisoners in his group who started the march, only thirty-two were still alive when they reached Czechoslovakia on March 12, 1945.

The Liberators

After their experience in Majdanek, the Russians did not emphasize the horrors they found when they liberated Auschwitz on January 27, 1945, or in the subsequent camps at Sachsenhausen, Ravensbrück, Stutthof, and Theresienstadt. It was not until the British, Canadian, and American troops began liberating camps in April and May that the world started to believe that the Nazis had killed hundreds of thousands—perhaps millions—of people. On April 15, British and Canadian troops arrived at the Bergen-Belsen concentration camp in Germany. They found sixty thousand prisoners still alive and thousands of corpses rotting in the open air. Between starvation and a typhus epidemic that was ravaging the camp, almost half of those prisoners who were alive on April 15 were dead within a few weeks. Robert Daniell was a British tank commander who could not believe the hell he had stumbled into: "There was a huge trench with probably 3,000 corpses in it. Putrefying bodies give off gases which make the bodies move and the pile was heaving as if the dead were alive."[26]

The Americans found the situation in Dachau, Buchenwald, Mauthausen, and other camps throughout German-occupied Europe much the same. The prisoners were barely alive, so skeletal that their backbones could be seen from the front of their bodies. They were covered with human waste, and the stench—from both those who were alive and those who were dead—was nearly unbearable. The Americans were so appalled and horrified by what they saw that they took their revenge on SS soldiers and guards still in the camps. According to one American soldier, "The men were deliberately wounding guards that were available and then turned them over to prisoners and allowed them to take their revenge on them."[27]

Generals Dwight Eisenhower, Omar Bradley, and George Patton insisted on seeing the camps themselves so that they could personally attest to the atrocities committed there. Concerning the hastily buried bodies of prisoners near Dachau, Patton ordered, "I want no American soldier digging for these bodies. Round up the town *Bürgermeister* [mayor] and whatever civilians are available and have them commence digging."[28] The Americans brought in thousands of local Germans to visit the camps and view the evidence of the mass murder. To the fury and disbelief of the Americans, most German civilians claimed they knew nothing about the camps or the conditions of the prisoners. Warren Dunn, a liberator of the Dachau concentration camp, asked them, "How could you not know? The stench from the crematorium must have told you something was going on there; the trains in the middle of the night bringing dead bodies to the crematorium—how could you not know?" To which they replied, "We didn't dare to even think that something like that was going on."[29]

The World's Response

Most of the world had a similar response when they discovered the extent of the Holocaust. Yet reports of atrocities committed against the Jews had leaked out of the death camps for years. Stories about the extermination camps and the horrors committed against the inmates had been printed by such notable newspapers as *The New York Times* and the London *Daily Telegraph* since 1942.

International organizations tried unsuccessfully to persuade the Allies to take steps to stop the genocide. In August 1944, the World Jewish Congress requested that the United States bomb Auschwitz, or at least the railway spurs leading to the gas chambers and crematoriums. The organization made it clear that tens of thousands of Jewish prisoners had been the victims of mass murder in the death camp. However, Assistant Secretary of War John J. McCloy refused the request:

After a study, it became apparent that such an operation could be executed only by the diversion of considerable air support . . . now engaged in the decisive operations and would . . . be of such doubtful efficacy that it would not warrant the use of our resources.[30]

However, on July 7, 1944, American bombers had flown over the railroad leading to Auschwitz. Six weeks later, on August 20, 120 U.S. Army Air Force planes dropped bombs on the factory at Auschwitz-Buna, less than five miles east of Auschwitz-Birkenau. It was months before Allied armies would reach the camps. In that time, many more prisoners would perish. For them and the millions of prisoners that came before, the liberation of the camps in 1945 came too late.

Notes

1. Adolf Hitler, *Mein Kampf*. Trans. Ralph Manhein. New York: Mariner Books, 1999, p. 57.

2. Hitler, *Mein Kampf*, p. 58.

3. Hitler, *Mein Kampf*, p. 304.

4. Hitler, *Mein Kampf*, p. 327.

5. Hitler, *Mein Kampf*, p. 324.

6. Hitler, *Mein Kampf*, p. 679.

7. Quoted in Jeremy Noakes and Geoffrey Pridham, *Foreign Policy, War, and Racial Extermination,* vol. 3 of *Nazism, 1919–1945: A Documentary Reader.* Exeter, England: University of Exeter Press, 1988, p. 1049.

8. Quoted in Ernst Klee, Willi Dressen, and Volker Riess, eds., *"The Good Old Days": The Holocaust as Seen by Its Perpetrators and Bystanders.* Trans. Deborah Burnstone. New York: Konecky & Konecky, 1991, p. 69.

9. Quoted in Michael Berenbaum, *The World Must Know: The History of the Holocaust as Told in the United States Holocaust Memorial Museum.* Boston: Little, Brown, 1993, p. 105.

10. Quoted in Berenbaum, *The World Must Know,* pp. 112–13.

11. Quoted in Eugène Aroneanu, ed., *Inside the Concentration Camps: Eyewitness Accounts of Life in Hitler's Death Camps.* Trans. Thomas Whissen. Westport, CT: Praeger, 1996, p. 6.

12. Quoted in Aroneanu, *Inside the Concentration Camps,* p. 117.

13. Quoted in Claude Lanzmann, *Shoah: An Oral History of the Holocaust: The Complete Text of the Film.* New York: Pantheon, 1985, p. 125.

14. Quoted in Joshua M. Greene and Shiva Kumar, eds., *Witness: Voices from the Holocaust*. New York: Free Press, 2000, p. 118.

15. Anita Lasker-Wallfisch, *Inherit the Truth: A Memoir of Survival and the Holocaust*. New York: Thomas Dunne Books, 2000, pp. 71–72.

16. Olga Lengyel, *Five Chimneys: The Story of Auschwitz*. New York: Howard Fertig, 1983, p. 79.

17. Lucie Adelsberger, *Auschwitz: A Doctor's Story*. Trans. Susan Ray. Boston: Northeastern University Press, 1995, pp. 75–76.

18. Quoted in Aroneanu, *Inside the Concentration Camps*, p. 52.

19. Quoted in Aroneanu, *Inside the Concentration Camps*, p. 60.

20. Quoted in Aroneanu, *Inside the Concentration Camps*, p. 60.

21. Quoted in Aroneanu, *Inside the Concentration Camps*, p. 57.

22. Quoted in Berenbaum, *The World Must Know*, p. 183.

23. Quoted in Aroneanu, *Inside the Concentration Camps*, p. 140.

24. Quoted in Aroneanu, *Inside the Concentration Camps*, p. 138.

25. Quoted in Aroneanu, *Inside the Concentration Camps*, p. 138.

26. Quoted in Eve Nussbaum Soumerai and Carol D. Schulz, *Daily Life During the Holocaust*. Westport, CT: Greenwood Press, 1998, p. 273.

27. Quoted in Berenbaum, *The World Must Know*, p. 189.

28. Quoted in *The Holocaust Chronicle: A History in Words and Pictures*. Lincolnwood, IL: Publications International, 2000, p. 604.

29. Quoted in Steven Spielberg and Survivors of the Shoah Visual History Foundation, *The Last Days*. New York: St. Martin's Press, 1999, p. 228.

30. Quoted in Berenbaum, *The World Must Know*, p. 145.

Chapter 1

Arrival

Chapter Preface

The core belief of Adolf Hilter's Final Solution—the extermination of all European Jews—was that the Jews were *untermenschen* (subhuman). This gave the Nazis the justification they needed for their actions against the Jews. As part of the final step in Hitler's plan to murder the Jews, the Jews were deported in cattle cars to labor and concentration camps. As many as eighty to a hundred people were crammed into a boxcar in which they traveled for days with no food, water, windows, toilet facilities, or way to care for the sick and dying. When they arrived at the camps, they were called "pigs" by the guards because of the filthy conditions over which they had no control. The travelers were beaten and families were separated; the very young, the very old, and the sick were immediately murdered, either shot or sent to the gas chambers.

Those who managed to avoid the first selection for extermination were ordered to leave the few possessions they had managed to bring with them. They were then forced to strip completely naked in front of leering guards. From there they were squeezed into a shower room, where they endured a brief ice-cold shower, then a spray of insecticide to delouse them. Next the prisoners were herded into another room where barbers waited to completely shave them with clippers that tore the hair, beards, mustaches, and pubic hair from their bodies. Afterward, they stood outside, still naked, often for hours regardless of the weather, before they were given shoes and used, filthy clothing. In some camps, the prisoners received a numbered tattoo, usually on their left arm, and were told they no longer had a name. After all this, the prisoners were barely recognizable—even to those who knew them well—as the same people who had arrived just a short time before.

The Train Ride to Auschwitz

Rena Kornreich Gelissen

Rena Kornreich Gelissen had been sent by her parents to live with family and friends in Czechoslovakia and Austria to escape the Nazi regime in Poland. Tired of running, Gelissen was twenty-one years old when she obeyed the German order to turn herself in to work in a labor camp. She was on the first transport of Polish Jews to the notorious extermination camp of Auschwitz in western Poland. She and her sister Danka managed to survive there for more than three years, an incredible achievement when most inmates died from starvation, disease, or gassing after just three or four months in the camp.

In the following essay, Gelissen recounts the miserable conditions inflicted on the Jews from the moment they arrived at the train station to be deported to "work camps." Instead of being transported in passenger cars, she describes how the Jews were crowded into cattle cars with no seats, windows, food, water, or toilets. Several people in her boxcar died during the journey and the passengers were forced to keep the dead bodies with them for the duration of the journey. By the time they reached their destination, they no longer felt human and some were close to losing their minds.

At the railway station there are hundreds of men, women, and children standing in line. There are many girls about my age. What is going on? Why are children being sent to work? What am I doing here? I am supposed to be

Excerpted from *Rena's Promise*, by Rena Kornreich Gelissen with Heather Dune Macadam. Copyright © 1995 by Rena Kornreich Gelissen and Heather Dune Macadam. Reprinted by permission of Beacon Press, Boston.

getting married, not going to a labor camp. I have to remind myself that I am doing the right thing, but reality is not a comfort.

Word has spread quickly through the town of Hummene (Czechoslovakia) that there are Jews being shipped off to work camps today. Our people shout encouragement while standing by the station gates throwing oranges to those of us being loaded onto the train. I catch a few, sticking them in my handbag. For a moment I scan the crowd, looking for a familiar face; I do not know if I should be sad or happy that there is no one waving to me.

A Rude Shock

When one thinks of a train ride, one imagines benches, or at least seats, or, if one has a little money, perhaps a berth. It is obvious, however, that the cars they are loading everyone into are for animals—cattle cars, to be exact.

"Where are we supposed to sit?" The people around me voice their outrage. "This is not a train for people!" No one is listening as eighty of us are piled into the car. It is standing room only. We step on each others toes, apologize, then step on someone else's.

There's a steady buzz of dismay over our plight. The lady next to me is nursing her baby. She is not a Jew, she is a communist.

"Would you like an orange?" I ask.

"I didn't know I needed to bring food or clothing," she says in Slovakian. I tear off a piece of challah and place a piece of precious chocolate into her hands.

"Bless you, bless you." Her voice breaks from dryness; I wish I had water to quench our thirst. The train starts with a lurch. There is nothing to lean against but the next person.

"Where's the toilet?" someone asks. There is a bucket which is supposed to be a toilet. Hours go by before an embarrassed elder woman has to use "the facilities." Her daughter holds up her coat as a screen while the lady tries to squat on her shaky legs.

"I'm sorry," she apologizes, "I could not hold myself any longer." Some people are shocked, hiding their eyes in shame, but sooner or later everyone must follow suit or mess themselves. It has become apparent that this will not be a short journey, and before the day is out excrement slops freely over the edge.

We expect someone to come dump our refuse for us. Every time the train stops, the ones closest to the door pound against its indifference, yelling, "Open the door! The smell is killing us!"

No one answers our cries. The train moves again. There is no relief.

Death on the Train

Somebody dies. We try to move away from the corpse, but there's no place to go. I have never been so close to death. I pray for his eyes to blink and flicker once more. A thin wail rises up out of the belly of the woman whose husband has passed. Lamentations. My bones resonate with her voice. Staring at her mouth, I am amazed at how such sounds of pain and sorrow can emanate from such a small place. She begins to panic. "What will happen to me?" she askes us in Yiddish. "Why has my husband died?" No one can answer her questions. She cradles his head against her bosom, speaking to him as if he can hear her.

Another person dies. There is sobbing, then shocked silence. I stare at the bodies. They can't be dead. They are sleeping and will wake up. I wait for the nightmare to end. If they're not going to wake, surely I will. It is a chant in my head: they can't be dead. It's impossible. This is just supposed to be a train ride to a work camp, not an ordeal. The bodies never move.

Someone pounds against the door. "Please help us!" Others join him. "Someone has died! Please, let us remove the dead." There is no sitting shiva, no one to say the Kaddish. There is a prayer, but we have no rabbi with us. Our faith dangles before us. We cannot prepare the bodies properly.

We cannot honor their passing. We are too afraid for our own lives. The train stops again and again. We pound and plead for mercy, but the voices outside ignore us.

Losing Track of Time

Is it days or is it hours?

The door opens. For just a split second, daggers of light blind us. Like wild animals caught by a farmer's lantern, we freeze immobile and in shock. The air saturates our lungs. We have forgotten what fresh smells like—gentle and sweet, not acrid, as the car has become.

"Throw out your dead!" The orders are immune to our pain.

Bodies are tossed out as unceremoniously as the bucket, which is also dumped. The door slams shut too quickly, severing the outside world from our senses. Now that we have something to compare it to, the closeness is more suffocating than before. The train continues its endless trek.

This journey is a blur in my mind. I have no idea if it is three days or five days since I wrote my letters to Danka and [Rena's fiancé] Schani. I begin to wish I could change my mind and go into hiding. I wish I could send a letter to Danka warning her. I have made a terrible mistake. I cannot think about that—there is no turning back.

There is no more food to nosh on. There never has been any water to drink. Nothing is left to relieve the growing ulcers in our stomachs.

They are not expert at shipping human cargo yet. The stops are so many I give up trying to count them, reserving my energy for more important things. My mind is as heavy as wet sand shifted through a net of unconscious daze. I think about nothing.

Poland

The woman feeds her baby. The voices around me share stories. I have nothing to share. Somewhere in the lapse of time I hear somebody say, "Is anyone here Polish?"

I do not answer at first. It takes time to register what my ears have heard. Looking across the dingy compartment of strangers, I remember. "I'm Polish!"

"Can you read the signs we're passing?" The men in our car lift me up so I can see the signs along the tracks through the barred window high above our heads.

The wind whips across my eyes. I blink back the pain as I recognize my native tongue, my native land. "We're in Poland," I say from high above their heads.

"Where are they bringing us?" Speculation and theories are discussed, but mostly there are just more questions.

"What are they doing?" Our voices ice the air.

Then there is nothing but the sound of wheels against tracks, tracks against wheels; even the baby has stopped crying.

It is as if I am in a tunnel with no light at the end and nothing to stop the onslaught of darkness. The faces around me have changed over the days until no one is far from losing control of their minds. It is as if the world has been shorn of all color, the only hues in the spectrum being black, gray, and the white of my boots. In this dank and fetid car I determine what I must do to survive. Everything that reminds me of what once was—my childhood, my past, my life—must be locked away in the recesses of the unconscious, where it can remain safe and unmolested. The only reality is now. Nothing else can matter.

Old and Sick to the Left, Healthy to the Right

Leo Fettman

In March 1944, Leo Fettman was nineteen when he and his family were given ten minutes by the Nazis in Hungary to gather their belongings together before they were sent to a ghetto. A month later, the Fettmans were in a cattle car on their way to Auschwitz where most of his family was murdered.

In the following excerpt, Fettman describes the scene after his family arrived at the train station at Auschwitz. Children told to remain in the boxcars were shot by the Nazis, and the ill and extremely elderly were loaded onto Red Cross vans and gassed in the vans. Those remaining were subjected to an ominous selection; some were sent to a line on the left, while others were motioned to another forming on the right. None of the new arrivals knew the significance of being sent to one side or the other. Fettman's father, mother, and grandmother were all directed to the left side, which led to the deadly gas chambers. Fettman and his brother were on the right; they went to the showers and the camp to survive another day.

Fettman was soon sent to a labor camp nearby to work. He was in the camp hospital with a broken leg when the Russians liberated the camp in May 1945. Fettman now lives in Nebraska and is a cantor in his synagogue.

Excerpted from *Shoah: Journey from the Ashes: A Personal Story of Triumph over the Holocaust,* by Leo Fettman as told to Paul M. Howey (Omaha: Six Points Press, 1999). Copyright © Leo Fettman, 1999. Used with permission.

W e had been trapped inside this coffin on rails for two days and two nights. In some ways, it felt as though it had been an eternity. On the other hand, I was afraid for the journey to end for fear that what awaited us might even be worse, although that seemed inconceivable. It made no difference. We had lost all control of our lives as we continued to be propelled toward some unknown destination and fate.

"We are taking you to a better place." Another lie from another grinning Nazi guard who was standing outside our boxcar at one of the many stops. *Was there any reason to have hope?* They had rousted us from our homes, imprisoned us in the ghetto behind barbed-wire fences, and now they had crammed us into these miserable cattle cars.

The shrill whistle of the locomotive once again pierced the air. And again! Had we arrived at last? Were we soon to be free of this hell? I could see only desolate, treeless plains through the small opening near the roof.

Then I saw it. There was a gigantic iron gate archway bearing a sign that read *Arbeit Macht Frei* in large letters. *Work Makes Freedom.* The train passed through this gate.

The Last Stop

The whistle screeched one last time as the train moved into a railway station to disgorge its pitiful cargo. The heat was so oppressive that it stung my eyes and made the steel surrounding us unbearably hot. I could hardly breathe. The train came to a sudden stop, one car hitting another. Once again, we were thrown into the people standing next to us, releasing renewed whimpers and wailing. Last stop! We had arrived. Where, we did not know.

From what little I could see from my vantage point, the landscape appeared gray and dead. I saw the silhouette of what looked like a factory. A large, brick smokestack belched towering black plumes into an already leaden sky. Red and yellow tongues of flames licked angrily through the top of the chimney. In the foreground were long rows of barbed-wire fencing interrupted every hundred meters or so by guard towers with large searchlights. I could make out groups of uniformed prisoners shuffling along inside the fence. They looked more dead than alive. A strange odor of decay hung in the air.

Down the line ahead of us, we could hear the boxcar doors opening and the commands of the Nazi officers as they shouted over the frantic conversations and the screams of the thousands upon thousands who were still entombed in the boxcars. My stomach churned. I tried to lose myself in prayer. *From the depths I called You. My Lord, hear my voice, may Your ears be attentive to my pleas. Give me strength to endure!*

The Doors Are Opened

We were alerted by the sound of the soldiers' boots as they approached. Everyone in the boxcar fell silent as the heavy door rumbled open. I was standing near the door and could see hundreds of confused, frightened people already standing on the platform alongside the train. Nazis armed with sticks and growling dogs surrounded them. A soldier with a bullhorn blared the orders: "All children and elderly must remain inside the car! Children and elderly remain inside the car! The rest may disembark. Jump out or get out now!"

As my fellow prisoners began to exit, I glanced back and saw to my horror lifeless bodies collapsing on the floor of the boxcar. About one-third of people had died during the trip. We were packed so tightly together that the dead had had no space to fall. No one knew.

The odor of the corpses swirled together with the fumes from the excrement and urine inside. The heavy air outside gave little relief as I jumped onto the platform. I looked around for my father, my mother, my grandmother, and my brother. I found them. They were all alive. Filthy, but alive. We stood shoulder to shoulder on the platform.

Then each of us was handed a postcard that read: "We have arrived safely at our destination. The Germans have treated us well. Our stay here should be pleasant and productive. Will write more later." There was a blank space for our signatures. On the threat of being shot, we were ordered to address the postcards to relatives and sign them. To whom could I send these lies? Nearly all of my immediate family members were with me. I filled in the name of a distant uncle, wrote a fictitious address, then added my signature. The postcards were collected.

Welcome to Auschwitz

Then a tall Nazi stepped up onto a small platform and looked down at us with a cold smile. His uniform was impeccable. His evil seemed impenetrable. He carried a swagger stick with which he punctuated his remarks. He spoke in German, and his words were immediately translated into several different European languages.

"My name is Dr. Josef Mengele. Welcome to Auschwitz, ladies and gentlemen." That was the time we found out that we were in Auschwitz. A shiver ran through the crowd. Some had heard of this infamous murderer and of this terrible place.

"I want the men to walk over there and form a line five people in each row," said Mengele pointing with his swagger stick. "Women over there. Five people in a row." We went to the designated places.

Once more, the Nazi with the bullhorn announced, "All children and elderly must remain on the train!" Mengele then assigned one soldier to each boxcar to remove the children. They grabbed the youngsters and babies by their arms, by their hair, by their legs, by whatever they could, and they threw them off the train like bundles of trash. Many other Nazis stood on the platform of the train station ready to catch the infants. Then they tossed some of the little ones into the air and began using them for target practice. I saw dozens and dozens of babies in the air all at one time.

I listened with horror to the staccato of the bullets from machine guns and rifles as they pierced soft tissue. Some of the SS caught the falling infants on their bayonets as part of this gruesome game. I saw a mother who recognized her child being thrown into the air, and she ran to her child. The mother and child were gunned down together. I witnessed the Nazis' delight in this game of death, which ended with the dead or mortally wounded children being thrown into a bloody pit. This is not something I saw on television or that I made up! I was there. I saw it. It is a horrible, horrible picture that is burned indelibly in my mind. I wish I could forget it; but, for many reasons that will become clear, I should not.

The Infirm and the Elderly

Next, the infirm and the extremely elderly were loaded onto Red Cross trucks. There were many, many Red Cross trucks. They filled up the trucks with these people. They drove only a short distance. The drivers got out, climbed on top of the trucks, and dropped cannisters through openings in the roofs. They were gassing the people right in the Red Cross trucks. You could hear them screaming, but only for a moment. Then they were forever silent.

To the Right or the Left

Mengele came back to where we were standing, still in rows of five. My father and brother were at my side. Mengele approached us, still smiling, and explained softly, "I am going to separate you now. I will walk among you. If I send you to the right, go to the right. If I send you to the left, go left." He stood before each of us for a split second, examining us from head to toe with his penetrating eyes. Now he pointed with his stick. *"Right, left, rechts, links, rechts, links."* And thus was our fate determined. Every task the Nazis performed was done in a most orderly and efficient manner.

We tried to figure out what was the difference between going to the right and going to the left. As we watched, it seemed that young people under sixteen and adults over fifty or so were being sent to the left, the others to the right.

Sandor and I were sent to the right. My father was sent to the left. I am certain that my mother and grandmother also were sent in that direction from the women's lines, although I couldn't see them. This was called the "selection."

I was standing next to Rabbi Fish from our shtetl. He was selected to go to the right. However, he begged the Nazis, "Can I go to the left?"

"You want to go to the left?"

"Yes."

"If you wish, certainly," Mengele grinned. "Go to the left."

Why did he want to go to the left? Perhaps, since he saw the women, the young, and the old being sent to the left, he assumed that he would not be required to do heavy labor. Our rabbi had devoted his life to prayer, Torah study, and good deeds we call *mitzvot*. He was not accustomed to manual labor. Who had any idea of the gravity of his request?

The Showers

Mengele then went over to those who were sent to the left and said to them, "You must be tired after such a long journey. You are filthy. We want you to be more comfortable, so please take off your dirty clothes. You are permitted to keep your glasses, but nothing else. You will take showers to delouse yourselves and then receive clean uniforms."

Quietly and obediently, they followed his directions, arranging their clothes in neat piles at their feet. Indeed, they were dirty, and they were covered with lice. Still, I suspected this was just another way to humiliate us. A cluster of Nazis took photos and movies of them as they undressed. The Nazis were taking photographs constantly.

Once they had removed their clothes, the rumor in the camp later was that they were given small bars of soap with the initials R.J.F. (*Rein Jüdisch Fett*—Pure Jewish Fat) carved into them. There is some debate as to whether this soap actually existed. I don't know for certain. I do know that, having seen the barbaric acts of the Nazis, it would not have surprised me.

They clutched the bars of soap in their hands and began to move slowly along the cinder path toward the bathhouse. How did they know it was a bathhouse? They presumed it was because the Nazis had placed a sign that read "Baths and Disinfecting Room" in Hungarian, German, French, and Greek over the door.

At that moment, a small orchestra began playing some rather oddly cheerful music. The degradation, the brutal murders, the stench, and now the music—it was so incongruous, so surreal. I had to shake my head to make certain this was all not some terrible dream.

I watched as my parents walked through the door of the bath building. That was the last time I saw my parents.

Once they were all inside—there must have been 2,000 people crowded in there—the doors were sealed shut behind them. We soon heard the most awful sounds coming from the building. We realized then that this was a gas chamber. The people inside were crying, shouting, and singing. Yes, singing. They were singing the well known prayer *Ani Maamin* (I Believe in G-d). I turned to my brother and said, "They are murdering them, aren't they? They are murdering our people, and our people still believe in G-d?"

"Hell," I continued, "what G-d?" That was the first and last time that I ever questioned G-d. A short while later, wagons piled high with naked, lifeless bodies emerged from the building and disappeared around the corner. We had no time to absorb the magnitude of what we had just witnessed, however. Nor did we have even a moment to grieve.

The First Day

Sara Tuvel Bernstein

Sara Tuvel Bernstein was twenty-six when she arrived at
Ravensbrück concentration camp in northern Germany in the
fall of 1944. With her were her younger sister Esther, and two
friends, Lily and Ellen. In the following essay, Bernstein recounts their first day in a concentration camp. She describes
how the women were forced to undress completely in front of
male guards and then suffered the humiliation of having all
their body hair shaved. They were given rags to wear, fed a
thin soup, and sent to their barracks where they slept on
wooden bunks with no blankets. The next morning, the
women stood for hours during a roll call and watched as
guards carried out of the barracks the bodies of women who
had perished overnight.

Bernstein, Esther, Lily, and Ellen survived Ravensbrück
and were among those forced to evacuate when the Allies
closed in on the camp in January 1945. The inmates were
marched to the concentration camp in Dachau in southern
Germany. Lily died along the way, but Bernstein, Esther, and
Ellen all survived the war.

"*Nach Rechts! . . . Nach Links! . . . Nach rechts! . . .
Nach links! . . .*" a woman guard was ordering as we
approached the building; alternate lines of women were being sent to the right and to the left. Our line went to the
right, the four of us and twenty-five or thirty other women
entering a large, open room with low wooden benches all
along one wall. The air was chilly, the floor damp, shallow

puddles here and there darkening the cement. While we were nearly beyond thirst after weeks of being deprived of almost all water, for an instant I visualized sprawling on the floor, lapping up the few drops of water with my tongue.

"Achtung! Achtung!" a voice began shouting. I turned to look in the direction which the voice was coming from. A person wearing blue-gray pants and a jacket with a green triangle and bar sewn on the sleeve was speaking. The soldiers of the German National Guard who had accompanied us on the train and during the march into the camp had evidently turned us over to these camp guards.

Prepare for a Bath

"Achtung!" the voice commanded again. While the voice was deep and harsh, the face was soft, intriguing; I could not tell whether a man or a woman was speaking. We were ordered to form lines and to undress completely for a bath.

"A bath!" Ellen whispered to me. "I can't believe it."

Neither could I. The accumulated grime and dust had by now so mingled with the secretions of our bodies that the creases in our necks, wrists, and ankles held solid lines of dirt embedded into the skin.

What was the most disheartening, however, was my hair. Since I was seven or eight I had washed it often, immensely enjoying combing out the wet strands and letting them dry on my back into a flowing mass of waves. Now my hair protruded from my head in thick, twisted coils, matted and oily. When I tried to comb it with my fingers I was stopped by tangled snarls. *Maybe they will even give us combs,* I thought, picturing my hair soft and sweet-smelling once more.

The women began to undress, glancing quickly at the guards as they unbuttoned their blouses and slipped off one sleeve. We were ordered to fold our coats, pants, blouses, sweaters, skirts, socks, and underwear and place them in piles at our feet. Our shoes were to be set to one side. When I had finished undressing I was so cold that I could not stop shivering. The windows were broken and the wind was blowing in on us in strong gusts. Glancing around the room covertly, I saw one girl with trembling arms crossed over her breasts while another was bent over, arms folded tightly together. Several women still held on to the last piece of clothing they had taken off—an undershirt, a white pair of underpants—and draped it over the lower part of their bodies. The two guards stood together in the front, arms around each other's waists.

"Beeilen Sie sich!" shouted one of the guards. As I understood German, I realized that she was telling us to hurry. Most of the women, however, spoke only Hungarian and could only guess what they were being ordered to do. One by one the women still holding on to a piece of clothing met the narrowed eyes of a guard staring at them and let the garment fall.

No More Hair

Two more guards wearing the same uniform entered the room, one carrying scissors, the other a bowl of water and a razor. Walking up to the first row of women, the guard with the scissors grabbed the hair of the woman first in line with her left hand; with the right she made one quick cut at the base of the neck. A mass of black hair fell away. The guard walked to the front of the room, threw the shorn-off hair on a bench, and went back to the same woman. Her scissors moved quickly; here, there, and there a chop was made. Disparate tufts stuck out in one place while in another the hair was cut so close that the whiteness of the scalp was visible.

The guard moved on down the line of women in front of me, making separate piles in front of the room: one for blond hair, one for brown, one for chestnut, one for black.

When the guard reached our row she quickly slashed off Ellen's hair, Esther's, and Lily's; I was next. She grabbed me with a hard yank that hurt deeply, as if she were pulling my hair out by the roots, and then paused for a minute.

"Just look at this!" she yelled.

Who is she talking to? I wondered. The women in front of me turned around to look.

The guard with the razor walked over to us from the opposite end of the room. Her hands were covered with curly hair. "Hah!" she laughed. "Isn't she a fine one!"

The first guard took her scissors and made several quick, sawing movements. My hair fell into her hand. Four more rapid snips were made around my head and finally the guard walked to the blond pile and threw my hair on it with a careless toss. It began to slide from the top of the pile, slowly at first, and then, picking up speed, tumbled to the floor, landing in front of the bench. The guard, going by with a length of black hair, gave it a kick with her boot.

Humiliation

A hot burning stung my eyelids. Tears gathering behind them pushed out in clusters, collected in the lower portions of my eyes. I could not pull my gaze away from my hair. Finally I forced myself to look at the other women huddled into themselves, shivering, diminished, like sheep after a shearing. One woman had no hair at all except for a tuft sticking straight up from the top of her head. Another had a short stubble over one ear, a longer layer above the other. I could only guess at my own appearance but I imagined jagged lines, ragged edges.

As I stood there, drawn deep inside myself, the other guard approached and ordered me to spread my legs apart. My body obeyed, my mind remained dark, numbed. I felt a sharp pull on my pubic hairs followed by a biting pain as the razor made two, three swipes across. The guard moved on, swishing her razor in a bowl of water black with hair, traces of red floating on the dirty scum. I looked at my legs. A trickle of blood was easing down the inside of one calf. *I would almost rather die than suffer this,* I thought, and crept back into the softness inside my head.

Clothing

The piles of clothes at our feet were picked up and put into large bins at one end of the room. A few minutes later

wooden crates were brought into the room and a guard began to move down the rows. Each woman was handed an
undershirt, regardless of its size. I was given a gray, soiled
piece of thin cotton that hung to my feet. Next the guards
came down the rows with crates of dresses; again we were
given whichever piece of clothing was closest to the guard's
reach. A dark green jersey dress, the kind of garment an
older woman might have worn to an afternoon tea in Bu-
dapest, was thrust at me. Across the front and the back were
large stripes made of a dark cloth and sewn on so that a
large X was made across both my chest and back. All of the
other dresses bore the same markings. It slid over my head
and fell about my ankles, the waist coming almost to my
knees, slippery and cool on my body. I began to shake,
trembling violently, moving my hands up and down my
arms, trying to warm them. Lily, who was standing immediately to my right, must have touched Esther beside her and
pointed to me; Esther and I never lined up directly next to
each other for fear that we would be recognized as sisters
and separated.

"Are you all right?" Esther whispered across to me.

I nodded my head, glancing at her. I was relieved to see
that she had been given a woolen dress. The right sleeve was
torn, the midriff was soiled, and there were several holes in
the skirt, but it would be warm.

Everything Is Gone

The guards came through again, handing out coats. I could
not understand at first why they took away all of our clothes
only to give us in return garments that must have been worn
by other women entering the camp. But as I looked around
at the women beside me withdrawn into their meager, worn
rags, I saw that we were no longer the strong women who
had been able to endure hard labor, wartime conditions, and
separation from our families and friends. The shearing of our
heads and vulvas, the stealing of our clothes and everything
we had owned, took from us the last traces of who we had

been. My knapsack on the train, my mother's chains and rings, would never be given back. I felt their loss almost as much as the loss of my hair. All I had left was Samuel's ring.

When the guard reached me she held out a long gray coat. Without thinking I took it from her with my right hand. Immediately the guard circled the ring with her fingers and thumb, giving it a hard yank. My finger felt as if it were being pulled from me. The ring would not come off. Her grip tightened; the flesh around the ring was squeezed tightly. I cried out in pain.

"Quiet!" she hissed.

Again she pulled, spitting on the ring twice while she wiggled it back and forth. Finally, in one smooth movement, she scraped it over the ridge of my knuckle and slipped it off the end of my finger and into her pocket. Quickly she glanced around. Satisfied that no one had seen her, she shoved her crate of coats forward and moved on. . . .

Colored Triangles

The two guards who had marched us into the room and remained standing at the front, now moved apart. One began to speak to us in German.

"You are in Ravensbrück, an all-women camp. There are no men here except for a few doctors in the hospital. You are our first Jewish prisoners. We have honored you by giving you the Star of David." The speaker glanced quickly at the other guard, barking a short laugh.

"Every woman is in here for a reason," she continued. "The color of the triangle on the sleeve will tell you what it is: criminals have green triangles; prostitutes, purple; those arrested for political or religious reasons, red; and Jew bitches like you, yellow. In case you're wondering why I'm here, you can see by my triangle that I'm a criminal. Does anyone want to know what I did?"

No one made a sound. The realization that she was a woman and a criminal as well was more than we could absorb at one time.

"Well, I'll tell you anyway," she went on. "I killed someone . . . stabbed her with a knife! Anything else you want to know?"

Again there was silence.

"From now on," she continued, "each of you will be known by your number. Each of you will be accounted for twice a day. We know exactly how many of you there are by the numbers."

I looked down at my sleeve and again read the number: 85803.

"From here you will be taken to barracks twenty-one and given supper. Tomorrow morning you will begin work. Now, put your shoes back on. Quickly!"

She and the other guard began to move among us with long, slender poles, hitting the women who were bent over tying their shoelaces. The shoes were damp from the long walk through the forest and would not slide onto our bare feet. We were not going to get stockings, I realized, or underpants. We were not going to get a bath or even so much as a drop of water to drink. I tied my shoes in loose knots and stood up again before a guard reached me.

Ravensbrück

A few minutes later we were driven out of the building by the guards, who stood to one side, striking out randomly at the passing women with their poles. We came into a yard lit in areas by floodlights beaming down from the high walls and were marched between more long, gray buildings stretching out on both sides of us for as far as I could see—rows and rows of unpainted wood shacks with empty, black windows.

We stopped before the building marked "21" and were made to form a line outside. After a long wait in the wind each of us was ordered to remove her shoes and then allowed to enter a room immediately to the right of the large entrance hall. Here flush toilets were laid out in rows. All but one, however, were roped off. The line moved forward very slowly as each woman took her turn and then joined another line moving through the entrance room. As Esther, Lily, Ellen, and I passed through the toilet line and joined the second line, the comforting smell of hot soup and the warmth and light of the spacious room gradually eased through me. At last we were out of the cold. Surely now we would be given something to drink.

Tattooing

One of the enduring legacies for Jews who survived the Holocaust in concentration camps is the tattoo. Jews were the only prisoners in the camps who received a tattoo, although other prisoners were tracked through numbers on their uniforms. Olga Lengyel, who was sent to Birkenau in 1944, offers the following account of being tattooed in the camp.

In the camps of Auschwitz-Birkenau and, later, everywhere, many stories circulated about the tattooing of the prisoners. One would think that all the internees were tattooed upon arrival. Some believed the tattooing safeguarded one against being sent to the gas chamber, or that, at least, a special authorization from Berlin would be necessary before a registered-tattooed internee could be put to death. Even in our camp many were convinced of that.

Actually, as in so many matters, there was no fixed regulation. Sometimes all deportees were tattooed when they arrived. Then again there was laxity, and over a period of months the ordinary deportees were not tattooed at all.

The inmates of Birkenau were directed into their camps without matriculation numbers. Undoubtedly such formalities appeared superfluous even to the Germans, for these people were merely to be fuel for the crematory ovens.

As for the tattooings conferred upon the deportees, that was highly questionable. All who had some sort of responsibility, the blocovas and other minor officials and those who

Dinner

As we passed by a table, each of us was handed a metal cup and spoon. Ahead of us I could see a large pot of soup and a metal plate piled with bread. To be given something to drink at last, even if it was not cold water, was almost enough to take my mind off the despair that had been growing in me since we entered the camp. Finally I reached the soup and held out my cup. A woman prisoner, also with a

worked in the hospitals were tattooed. These were no longer "Haftling" but "Schutzhaftling" (protected prisoners). At the Schreibstube they received individual cards containing their names and other data. In case of natural death, the card had all the information. In case of execution, "S B," that is to say, "Sonderbehandlung" (special treatment), was added. Those who were not tattooed had no record of death in the files. They were no more than digits in the "production" statistics of the extermination plant.

The tattooing operation was carried out by the deportees employed at the "Politische Buro" (Political Bureau). They used a metal-tipped stylus. They inscribed the registration number on the skin of the arm, the back, or the chest. The ink which it injected under the skin was indelible.

When a tattooed person died, his registration number became "available" for the next deportee, since the Germans for some reason never went beyond the number 200,000. When they reached that point, they started over again with a new serial letter. The racial deportees had a triangle or a Star of David with their numbers.

The tattooing operation was painful and always was followed by inflammation and swelling. It is impossible to estimate the effect it had on morale. A tattooed woman felt that her life was finished; she was no longer anything but a number.

I was number "25,403." I still have it on my right arm and shall carry it with me to the grave.

Olga Lengyel, *Five Chimneys*. Chicago: Ziff-Davis, 1972.

green triangle on the sleeve of her uniform, dipped a ladle into the pot and held it above my bowl. Beside her stood another prisoner with a long fork, holding a plate with small pieces of meat. When a piece of meat was about to fall into my cup the prisoner with the fork picked it out of the ladle and put it on the plate of meat. My cup was filled with a few bits of turnip and clear broth.

Next another guard picked up a slice of dry, stale bread, splashed it with a spoon of pink liquid slightly resembling jam, and handed it to me. I followed the line, looking back to make sure that Lily, Esther, and Ellen were still behind me. Passing out of the entrance area, we continued down the large hallway which ran the length of the building and came to two doors, one on the right and one on the left. Another guard was standing near the doors and hitting the women as they passed by, yelling *"Achtung! Achtung!"*

The soup in the cups of the struck women splashed out and spilled onto the floor. This caused the guard to hit them again. Ducking away from her flailing pole, I squeezed against the far side of the door on the right and hurried through it. *If only the others follow me,* I thought. I looked back to see Ellen entering the room in the same way I had done, Lily and Esther following close behind her. There was no guard in sight here. The four of us moved together and looked around the room.

"This must be where we sleep," Ellen said.

"In those?" Lily asked.

The Barracks

We were in a cavernous room, dim and bitterly cold. A row of rickety wooden bunk beds three tiers high reached up above us. Every five tiers were nailed together so that a unit of fifteen beds were made. A narrow aisle ran between the units stretching as far as I could see in the pale light coming in from the hall. Other women had already crawled onto the row of bunks nearest us. A guard at the far end of the room began to shout, "Four to a bed! Four to a bed!"

"We better hurry," I said, "if we want to sleep together."

"Let's look on the far side of the room," Ellen said, beginning to run to the area next to the windows. We followed her and came upon a unit still completely empty. Lily sank into one of the beds on the bottom bunk.

"No, no," I said. "We're going up."

"I don't want to," Lily answered. "How can we even get up there? I don't see any ladders."

Rickety Bunks

"Look!" I said, grabbing one side of the beds. As I pushed against it very slightly, the whole set of fifteen beds rocked back and forth. Bits of straw from the second and third tiers rained down on the bottom tier. An icy wind, blowing in through the broken windows, picked up the falling straw and whipped it into our faces.

"But it will be too hard to climb up there," Lily said.

"Just put your foot on the bottom bed and pull yourself up to the next bed. In a minute you'll be on the top."

"But I'll spill my soup."

"Then drink it first. Up! Up!"

Esther went first, Lily second, Ellen third, and I last, the beds creaking and leaning precariously as we climbed. After a few minutes of turning, placing a foot so it did not stick into someone's side, or removing an arm from between two legs, the four of us were lying on the bed, two on each side, propped up on elbows and eating our bread. We had gulped down the cup of soup before we climbed up, yearning for ten, twenty more cups. The bread tasted like sawdust. A few minutes after we had finished a guard came through and told us to save the bread for the morning; it was our breakfast.

"Where are we?" Esther asked when the guard had passed by.

"I think we're in Germany—near Berlin maybe. We traveled very far north," I answered.

"Yes, but what is this place? What's happened to us?" she asked again.

"We're in a prison," I told her, "much worse than the one I was in before."

"The guards scare me," Lily said. "I've never seen women act like they do. I saw two of them kissing each other!"

"One of the German guards even killed someone!" Ellen said.

"Yes!" Lily answered. "I am so frightened. . . ."

Tears began to roll down her face, falling on the soiled blue coat she had been given. "Why did they have to cut off all our hair . . . even the hair. . . ." She began to cry louder, hiding her face in her hand.

We looked at each other in the half-light—at the naked heads, the bare necks, the big, terrified eyes. Each of us saw herself in the others and was ashamed. One by one we eased down onto the straw, the narrow, hard slats sticking out at both ends, and tried to lose ourselves in sleep. The cold found us lying exposed in the night with no blankets to cover us, no mattress under us—creeping up a leg, inside a coat sleeve, around a neck. We pressed to each other's backs and shoulders, trying not to think of the warm, soft comforters left on the train, of the beds we had once slept in beneath fresh sheets and thick blankets. . . .

The Next Morning

Sharp cries awoke me. "Don't hit me! Oh please," a woman in the next aisle was screaming.

"Get up, you Jew bitches!" a guard shouted in Polish. "Get up, pigs!" With each command her heavy, long stick came down on a bed of women with a whack. While I was still trying to struggle up from sleep, the guard was below us and striking at the women on the lower bunk. I shook Lily and then the other two. Quickly we slipped our tied-together shoes around our necks, grabbed our cups and spoons, and began to climb down the three tiers. The other women who were being herded toward the door pressed against us as soon as we reached the floor. I grabbed Lily's and Ellen's hands, Ellen grabbed Esther's, and the four of us joined the women rapidly surging out of the door, through the hallway past the entrance room, and outside into the ice-cold air. The sky was dark, the faintest traces of light only beginning to appear on the horizon.

Roll Call

"Zielappel! Zielappel! Schnell! Zielappel!" a guard began to shout. The first of hundreds of hours spent in counting us had begun. We were grouped into lines five across while the four guards who were in charge of our barracks counted. I stood in the dark, wondering how they could see to count, an arm's length from Lily on my left and Ellen on my right, Esther next to her. The air was clear, the stars above us sparkling dots of light in the blackness. A numbness began to creep through my fingers and I flexed and unflexed my hands inside the deep coat pockets. My feet suffered more; we were forbidden to move and could do no more than wiggle our toes back and forth inside our damp shoes. How I longed for my warm, woolen stockings and Samuel's slacks.

An hour must have passed as we stood there, silent, rigid, freezing cell by cell. One of the two German guards continued to count us. The other had already moved up and down our rows twice but had evidently come up with a different number each time. The counting continued through another hour, the sky turned a pale gray, then white, the cold entrenched itself firmly into our bodies, and still they were not finished with us.

Clearing Out the Dead

Across from us was the barracks where we had slept. As I was wondering how many hours more we would have to endure this, wondering how long we would be able to go on without slipping off to death like so many women before us, two guards came out of the door carrying something. I could not tell at first what it was, as their backs were turned to us. Then an arm fell, swayed back and forth as they walked. The body of a woman was thrown against the side of the barracks, hitting the rotting boards with a dull thud.

The guards returned with another body, throwing it down beside the first, and then another. As I watched, body after body was carried out, flung down, stacked into a pile in a pattern of horizontal lines repeated sixteen bodies high, five bodies long. I became almost hypnotized by the stacking of body upon body, the absence of any curves or angles, the endless piling up of long, faceless lines with only a slight resemblance to anything alive, anything human. Then, with a sudden shock, I thought, *They're women! Last night they went to sleep in the same building as I. This morning they're dead.*

The image of that pile of bodies frozen in the cold, gray light never left me. I would not be in that pile, I decided then. I would not die. Somehow, in whatever way I could, I would remain alive; Esther, Ellen, and Lily, as well. As long as I had strength we would live. I would see to it.

Chapter 2

Work Detail

Chapter Preface

M any concentration camps greeted new arrivals with a sign reading "*Arbeit Macht Frei*" over the entrance. The slogan, "Work Makes You Free," gave false hope to many Jewish arrivals who believed that they could indeed work for their freedom. Instead, the prisoners soon learned that, although they would work, they had very little chance of gaining their freedom.

For most of the inmates, the work they were assigned to do was hard, heavy labor. The Nazis used concentration camp prisoners to build and expand the very camps they were imprisoned in. Typical among the hard labor jobs were construction of buildings and roads, ditch digging, rock quarrying, and cutting and chopping wood. Occasionally, there would not be any work for the inmates to do; in those cases, the inmates would be forced to perform meaningless work, such as carrying stones from one side of a field to another and then back again. Most prisoners did not survive long if they were assigned to hard labor in the camps. The combination of dangerous jobs, brutal guards, and a starvation diet killed most workers within a few months.

Another job in which the workers lasted only a few months was the *sonderkommando*—the special work detail. These workers were the ones who dragged the dead bodies out of the gas chambers and carried them into the ovens in the crematorium. The *sonderkommando* workers were killed by the Nazis every two to three months and replaced with a new group of inmates.

There were a few work details that were highly coveted by the prisoners—anything inside out of the elements or working with food, such as in the kitchens or fields. Another highly desirable job was sorting the belongings of newly arrived prisoners; such a position allowed the sorters to steal money, gold, diamonds, clothing, food, and other valuables that they could then trade for food or other necessities. Some inmates worked as slave laborers in nearby factories. For the most part, these jobs were also welcome, because the inmates were sometimes able to make the acquaintance of civilian workers who might slip them some food or other contraband.

The Intellectual as Laborer

Jean Améry

Newly arrived prisoners were often quizzed by the Nazis at the concentration camps on their occupations. Young men and boys who claimed to be carpenters, electricians, masons, plumbers, and the like were frequently spared the first selection for the gas chambers. The camps were always in need of laborers and skilled craftsmen who could construct new buildings to enlarge the camp and provide goods and services needed by the guards and inmates. In addition, at some camps, prisoners who were machinists and other skilled laborers were sent to nearby factories to provide slave labor for the German war effort.

While skilled workers were usually valued by the Nazis, professionals, such as lawyers, accountants, teachers and professors, and sometimes doctors, were not. There was no place in the labor camps for these professions. Those who were not selected for the gas chambers as soon as they arrived at the camp were oftentimes chosen to perform hard labor, such as digging ditches or hauling rocks and railroad ties. A stated goal of the concentration camps was to work the inmates until they died from exhaustion, starvation, or beatings administered by the guards.

Jean Améry, a Jew and a member of the Belgian resistance, was incarcerated in Buchenwald, Bergen-Belsen, and Auschwitz from his capture in 1943 until the Allies liberated Auschwitz in the spring of 1945. In the following essay,

Excerpted from *At the Mind's Limits: Contemplations by a Survivor on Auschwitz and Its Realities*, by Jean Améry, translated by Sidney and Stella P. Rosenfeld. Copyright © 1980 Indiana University Press. Used with permission of the publisher.

Améry explains why intellectuals were at a disadvantage in the concentration camps, even when they managed to keep their profession a secret from the Nazis.

Consider the *external* situation of the intellectual, one that moreover was common to everyone else, including the nonintellectuals in the so-called higher professions. It was not a good situation, and it evidenced itself most dramatically in the question of the work assignment, which decided over life and death. The craftsmen in Auschwitz-Monowitz [an auxiliary camp at Auschwitz] were mostly assigned according to their trades, as long as—for whatever reasons that will not be discussed here—they were not gassed on the spot. A machinist, for example, was a privileged man, since he could be used in the planned IG-Farben factory and had the chance to work in a covered shop that was not exposed to the elements. The same holds true for the electrician, the plumber, the cabinetmaker, or carpenter. A tailor or a shoemaker perhaps had the good luck to land in a room where work was done for the SS. For the bricklayer, the cook, the radio technician, the auto mechanic, there was the slight chance of a bearable work spot and thus of survival.

Little Work for the Professional

The situation was different for the inmate who had a higher profession. There awaited him the fate of the businessman, who likewise belonged to the *Lumpenproletariat* of the camp, that is, he was assigned to a labor detail, where one dug dirt, laid cables, and transported sacks of cement or iron crossbeams. In the camp he became an unskilled laborer, who had to do his job in the open—which meant in most cases that the sentence was already passed on him. Certainly, there were also differences. In the camp chosen here as an example, chemists, for instance, were employed in their profession, as was my barracks mate Primo Levi from Turin, who wrote the Auschwitz book *If This Is a Man*. For physicians there was the possibility to find refuge in the so-called sick huts, even if it certainly did not exist for all. The Viennese physician Dr. Viktor Frankl, for example, who today is a world-renowned psychologist, was for years a ditchdigger in Auschwitz-Monowitz. In general, one can say

Factory Work

Germany's prisoners during the Holocaust worked not only in the camps, but also in nearby factories. Some of Germany's biggest industrial corporations—such as BMW, Daimler-Benz, Krupps, and IG Farben—used slave labor from concentration camps and some even built new factories to be close to the labor supply. The following excerpt, written by Benjamin B. Ferencz, a lawyer who, during the Nuremburg Trials, represented concentration camp survivors who sued German corporations seeking compensation for their slave labor, exposes some of the abuses suffered by the inmates who were forced to work in the factories.

From around the beginning of 1942 until the summer of 1944, when Allied bombing was effectively destroying German productive capacity, the demand for manpower from any source was overwhelming. No German company had to be coerced into taking labor. On the contrary, the firms had to use all their influence and persuasion to get all the help they felt they needed. The private companies were to pour millions of marks into the coffers of the SS for the privilege of using the camp inmates. An elaborate accounting system was set up to be sure that the companies paid the SS for every hour of skilled or unskilled labor and that deductions for the food provided by the companies did not exceed the maximum allowed. The inmates of course received nothing. They remained under the general control of the SS but under the immediate supervision of the companies that used them. The companies were required to see to it that adequate security arrangements, such as auxiliary guards and barbed wire enclosures, eliminated all possibility of escape. . . .

that at the work site the representatives of the higher professions were badly off. That is why many sought to conceal their profession. Whoever possessed even a bit of manual skill and perhaps was able to work with simple tools boldly declared himself a craftsman. To be sure, that meant

---

The conditions of work for the foreign laborers, the POWs, and the concentration camp inmates were reported by reliable witnesses after the war. It was well-known to all that the inmates were literally being worked to death. They were forced to run while unloading heavy cement bags weighing one hundred pounds. "If a prisoner collapsed at work," reported a British POW to the court at Nuremberg, "he was kicked and beaten in order to determine if he was still alive." Another testified that the inmates "were all starving to death. . . . If the German civilians saw us giving the soup (an inedible watery brew) to the inmates, they would kick it over." Inmates were forced to trot like dogs behind the bicycles of their amused German masters. Drinking water was contaminated, clothing was sparse, and the food totally inadequate. Many died of freezing or starvation. The conditions for all the forced laborers were terrible, but by far the worst were the conditions of the Jews. Five times as many Jews were crowded into the barracks as the number of ethnic German workers. Said another British soldier, "Of all the persons working at IG Auschwitz, the Jewish inmates had the worst time of it." "The German civilians often threatened the inmates that they would be gassed and turned into soap." "They looked on killing Jews as killing vermin." The I.G. Farben directors who visited the camp regularly and received all the reports were later to testify in their defense at Nuremberg that they never noticed anything was wrong, and besides, they were only carrying out orders and doing what was "necessary."

Benjamin B. Ferencz, *Less than Slaves: Jewish Forced Labor and the Quest for Compensation.* Cambridge, MA: Harvard University Press, 1979.

he was possibly risking his life, namely if it emerged that he had lied. The majority, in any event, tried their luck at playing themselves down. The gymnasium (high school) or university professor, when asked about his vocation, timidly said "teacher," in order not to provoke the violent rage of the SS man or the Kapo. The lawyer transformed himself into the plainer bookkeeper, the journalist perhaps passed himself off as a typesetter, in which case there was little danger that he would have to provide proof of his ability at this trade. And so the university professors, lawyers, librarians, economists, and mathematicians dragged rails, pipes, and construction beams. For these tasks they brought with them mostly little skill and but slight bodily strength, and only in rare instances did it take long before they were eliminated from the labor process and ended up in the main camp, where the gas chambers and crematories stood.

Camp Life and the Intelligentsia

If their situation at the work site was difficult, it was no better inside the camp. Camp life demanded above all bodily agility and physical courage that necessarily bordered on brutality. The intelligentsia were only seldom blessed with both, and the moral courage that they often tried to employ in place of the physical was not worth a trifle. Assume for a moment that we had to prevent a professional pickpocket from Warsaw from stealing our shoelaces. Circumstances permitting, an uppercut certainly helped, but by no means that intellectual courage through which perhaps a political journalist endangers his career by printing a displeasing article. Superfluous to say that only very rarely did the lawyer or gymnasium teacher know how to execute an uppercut properly; rather, he was far more often the receiver, and in taking it hardly more able than in giving it. In matters of camp discipline things were also bad. Those who on the outside had practiced a higher profession generally possessed little talent for bedmaking. I recall educated and cultivated comrades who, dripping with sweat, battled every morning with their straw mattress and blankets and still achieved no proper results, so that later, at the work site, they were plagued by the fear—which grew into an obsession—that on their return they would be punished with a beating or the withdrawal of food. They were up to neither bedmaking nor a brisk response to the command "Caps off!" and when the occasion arose, they were totally unable to find that mode of speech vis-à-vis the senior block inmate or the SS man that was both submissive and yet self-assured, and with which threatening danger could possibly be averted. In the camp, therefore, they were as little respected even by higher-ranked prisoners and comrades as they were at the work site by civilian laborers and Kapos.

Communication

Still worse: they didn't even find *friends*. For in most cases, it was physically impossible for them spontaneously to use the camp slang, which was the only accepted form of mutual communication. Modern intellectuals quarrel a great deal about their communication difficulties and in the process talk a lot of pure nonsense, which would better remain unsaid. Well, in the camp there truly was a problem of communication between the intellectual and the majority of his comrades. It presented itself hourly in a real and painful way. For the prisoner who was accustomed to a somewhat refined manner of expression, it was possible only with much effort to overcome his distaste for saying "Beat it!" or to address a fellow prisoner exclusively with "Hey, you." Only too well do I recall the physical disgust that regularly seized me when an otherwise quite proper and sociable comrade inevitably found no other form of address for me than "my dear fellow." The intellectual suffered from such expressions as "grub sarge" or "to organize" (which designated the illegal appropriation of some object); yes, even such set phrases as "to go on transport" he uttered only with difficulty and hesitatingly.

Survival

But now I have arrived at the basic psychological and exis-
tential problems of camp life and at the situation of the intellectual in the narrower sense outlined at the start. Reduced to its most concise form the question that arises is:
did intellectual background and an intellectual basic disposition help a camp prisoner in the decisive moments? Did
they make survival easier for him? . . . In Auschwitz the intellect was nothing more than itself and there was no chance
to apply it to a social structure, no matter how insufficient,
no matter how concealed it may have been. Thus the intellectual was alone with his intellect, which was nothing other
than pure content of consciousness, and there was no social
reality that could support and confirm it. The examples that
come to mind in this context are in part trivial; in part, however, they must be taken from realms of existence that can
scarcely be portrayed.

The Special Work Detail

Oscar Berger

Adolf Hitler's Final Solution to exterminate all the Jews and other undesirables in Europe presented a special problem in the death camps: what to do with the thousands and millions of dead bodies created as a result of the "special actions." In some camps the Nazis solved this problem by burning and burying the dead in huge pits while in other camps the dead were burned in crematoriums. Rudolf Höss, commandant of Auschwitz, bragged that the gas chambers in his camp were an improvement over those in Treblinka because each of Auschwitz's gas chambers could kill two thousand people at one time while Treblinka's ten chambers could only kill two hundred people each.

After the prisoners were killed in the gas chambers, the bodies had to be disposed of. This was the job of the *sonderkommando,* or "special work detail," who first shaved the dead of their hair and then searched the bodies for money, gold, diamonds, and other valuables. Then the workers transferred the bodies to the crematoriums or pits to be burned. In the death camps during World War II, the crematoriums *sonderkommando* had a life expectancy of about three months; the Nazis, in order to keep their genocide a secret from the outside world, killed the workers regularly and then replaced them with a new work detail. Oscar Berger is one *sonderkommando* who survived his deadly assignment. In the following essay, Berger describes the horror of watching innocent peo-

Excerpted from *The Buchenwald Report*, translated and edited by David A. Hackett. Copyright © 1995 by Westview Press, a member of the Perseus Books Group. Reprinted by permission of Westview Press, a member of Perseus Books LLC.

ple be murdered and then being forced to dispose of their bodies. Although Berger escaped from Treblinka in 1942, he was recaptured a few months later and sent to Auschwitz-Birkenau and later Buchenwald, where he remained until the Allies liberated the camp on April 11, 1945.

I was a merchant, living with my wife and son in Kattowitz [Katowice, Poland]. At the beginning of the war, we fled to Kielce, to my wife's parents. Without any reason, I was arrested by the Gestapo and jailed for four months. Repeated abuse was the order of the day: whippings, kickings, and bites by vicious watchdogs. After bribing a Gestapo agent, I was released.

In the Ghetto

In July 1942 the ghetto in Kielce was evacuated, and the ghetto residents were brought to Treblinka. We were transported in cattle cars, eighty to 100 persons jammed together in each car. Beatings by truncheons, rifle butts, and countless shootings were part of our treatment. The only luggage we were permitted was hand baggage. I was separated from my wife and never saw her again. Shortly before the evacuation of the ghetto, all sick persons were killed. That included those at home as well as in the hospital, in addition to residents of old people's homes and children in orphanages—a total of 400 to 500 people. The majority were killed through injections, the remainder through shooting.

As a strong, young person I was employed at Kielce in burying corpses in a large trench, inside a spacious garden on the Obrzejgasse on the grounds of a forester's house. About fifty to sixty Jews were occupied with this work. The corpses were thrown into the trenches fully clothed. We had to search through them for jewelry and gold and turn the valuables over to the SS, along with all the money we found. The corpses were covered with potash, the trenches covered over. As we worked, we were beaten and driven on by truncheons. Afterward we were herded into the synagogue, and Gestapo Chief Thomas chose a portion of us to be transported to Treblinka. I was one of those Jews. I know nothing of the fate of those Jews left behind in Kielce.

The transport was horrifying. We were jammed together in railcars; children cried; women became hysterical. Before being loaded onto the railcars, we were robbed of money and jewelry. At first some were shot because they did not immediately turn over their valuables. At the ghetto square we had stood from 4:00 in the morning until 4:00 in the afternoon; then came the transport to the railroad station and the loading onto railcars. The next day, at about 3:00 in the afternoon, we arrived at Treblinka. The railroad station had a large sign with the inscription "Work Camp Treblinka." From there the train drove onto a siding that went into the forest. I would estimate the distance at 2 to 3 miles.

At this final destination we were presented with a picture of terror and horror. Hundreds of corpses were lying around; in between were pieces of luggage, clothing, suitcases, all jumbled together. We were driven out of the railcars; SS and Ukrainian SS men climbed onto the roofs of the railcars and shot wildly and indiscriminately at the crowd. Men, women, and children wallowed in pools of blood. People screamed and cried. Those who were not struck down were driven over the piles of dead and dying into a square surrounded by barbed wire. Two wooden barracks flanked the open space.

The *Sonderkommando*

Along with some others, including a certain Gottlieb from Kielce, I was chosen to clean the railcars. As we worked, we could see that all participants in the transport had to squat on the ground. SS and Ukrainian SS men were posted on the roofs of barracks and mowed everyone down with their machine guns. In thirty to forty minutes, thousands of people were killed or wounded. Escape was impossible; only a few individuals managed to jump into an open well, at the bottom of which they were left lying with broken bones and cracked skulls, as I later saw for myself.

Along with several colleagues I had to pick up the corpses from the square and take them to a large trench that had been dug out by bulldozers. Whether dead or merely wounded, all were thrown into the trench. A "mercy shot" for the wounded was a rarity. From time to time the trenches were sprayed by machine gun fire; many corpse carriers lost their lives that way.

We were chased and driven on in our grim work by SS guards who had a drink in one hand and a truncheon or pistol in the other. Trembling from terror and agitation, thirsty, with shaking legs, half crazy from pain and fear, we had to complete our work with the most gruesome images before our eyes. Even now I am horrified by the memory of SS men grabbing small children by the feet and killing them by smashing them against tree trunks, often before the eyes of their sobbing and wailing mothers.

"Willner, bookkeeper with the Orion Firm in Kielce, can't go on; he requests a 'mercy shot' from the SS officer."

"What, with tits like that!" (We worked with bare chests.) "Don't you want to work anymore?" That was his reply, along with punches, beatings, and kicks. The man could not continue; finally the mercy shot came from a drunken Ukrainian.

We got nothing to eat, even though for weeks at a time the special work detail had to perform the same heavy, exhausting work. Two to three transports came in a day. We nourished ourselves with the food that we found in the luggage of the poor victims. We suffered terribly from thirst. At best we were allowed to drink water out of the well from which we had pulled the "escapees." Luggage, clothing, money, and jewels that we had to find and take out of the clothing were piled high in the warehouse. Goods worth millions were taken this way and stolen by SS men. Now and then a child managed to hide between the bundles of clothing and piles of luggage. Freedom did not last long, because by the next day at the latest, the children were punished by being thrown alive into the trenches between the corpses.

Among these came transports of corpses only. I suppose that these people were killed in the wagons by gas; I noticed no wounds. The bodies were twisted together; the skin was blue. Remarkably, it sometimes happened that small children from these transports, three- to five-year-olds, remained alive, though deaf and with glazed-over eyes, incapable of speech. We could not hide them long; after a short time they were discovered by the SS and killed off. There were also transports composed exclusively of children or old people. For hours they squatted on the square, only to be mowed down by machine gun fire.

Marked for Death

About our own fate we were clear. We were marked for death. For us there was neither pity nor any sort of favorable treatment. We lived completely cut off in small barracks. We carried the corpses to the trenches in a horse cart; if any of us became tired and sat on the cart, we were driven off by clubs and blows. Shooting, intended as punishment, was seen as liberation from our endless suffering. We were not only corpse carriers, but we also had to burn the corpses in the trenches. Wood was gathered, covered with a fluid, and lighted. The top layer of corpses melted together. I suppose that an exhumation would reveal corpses that were only half charred.

It often happened that I had to throw a wounded comrade into the grave. Their requests for a mercy shot remained unheard; I could not help them.

From time to time groups of 200 to 500 men from Treblinka work camp were driven naked into the woods. In rows and holding hands, as if they were in a circle dance, they were driven to the excavated trenches, where they were lined up on the edge. SS and Ukrainian guards made a sport of giving them the shot in the neck to send them to eternity. After the shootings they kicked the collapsing victims with their boot heels and amidst howls and cries argued over who had kicked a Jew the farthest. Anyone who succeeded in escaping during this sport was no longer granted the mercy of a shot in the neck; he was beaten to death.

In the weeks during which I worked at Treblinka, a small brick building was built on the other side of the forest. On the path to this building, a sign with the inscription "To the baths" was erected. Another sign demanded that all gold, money, currency, and jewelry be left in bundles at the window to the bath. From this time on new arrivals were no longer shot. Inside the enclosure men, women, and children had to take off all their clothes. Shoes had to be tied together in pairs. With clubbings, punches, and kicks, the victims were moved forward to the "baths." Those who were not quick enough were treated horribly. Usually the camp commandant together with his staff were present; he was the one who personally clubbed people to death. No one returned alive; they were gassed in the "baths."

A special work detail like ours took care of the burial or cremation of the corpses. We met people from this work detail because they did not receive food either, and we supplied them from the food we found in the luggage. The thirst that plagued all of us was so horrible that some individuals caught their own urine to at least wet their lips this way. We got the strength to carry out this terrible work from a comrade who constantly encouraged us to do our duty and perform this last service for our dead brothers and sisters, designated as the highest commandment of our faith.

Escape

A number of us made isolated attempts to escape. I belonged to the small number of lucky ones. Between blankets, bundles of clothes, and suitcases that we had to stack up in railroad cars, I hid together with a thirteen-year-old boy and my friend Gottlieb of Kielce. We took with us a generous amount of jewelry, gold, and money, mostly American dollars. Our escape succeeded in September

1942. The unfortunately too brief period of my freedom I used to inform Jews of the horrors of Treblinka and to advise them to hide.

I, too, tried to hide, but on January 5, 1943, my friend Gottlieb and I were arrested in Kraków as "partisans." After horrible tortures we had to confess that we were Jews. We were brought in shackles to the prison of the Jewish ghetto and remained there until March 14, 1943. Then we were taken along with 100 other Jews in closed vans to Auschwitz concentration camp and from there to Birkenau. Most were immediately separated out and gassed. Women were sent straightaway to the left, which meant gassing. But one woman threw herself at the feet of an SS officer and, as a strong person willing to work, begged to be allowed to remain in camp and work. She received permission to select some strong women and brought some with her. For the moment at least, they were saved and put into the women's camp.

A Nurse at Auschwitz

Olga Lengyel

Olga Lengyel, a surgical assistant who helped her husband
run a hospital in a city in Transylvania, arrived in Auschwitz
in 1944 and was soon assigned to work in the camp infirmary. In the following essay, she describes the conditions of
the hospital where she spent the remainder of the war. Although Auschwitz and other concentration camps had hospitals, most were hospitals in name only. Inmates were admitted only if they had a truly life-threatening disease or injury;
those with less severe illnesses were simply turned away.
Medical supplies, drugs, and sterile equipment were practically nonexistent. Few of the staff were actually trained
nurses and doctors but were inmates who volunteered for the
position for the better working conditions. Nazi physicians
who ran the hospitals used many of the patients in cruel and
sadistic experiments. In addition, the threat of selection hung
over all the admitted inmates in a hospital. The Nazis would
sweep through the hospital without warning on a regular basis and all patients would be taken off to the gas chambers,
regardless of their condition. Lengyel's parents, husband, and
children were all killed in Auschwitz.

For weeks there were no facilities for the care of the sick.
No hospital for health services had been organized and
no pharmaceutical products were available. One day we
were told that we were finally to have an infirmary. But here

again they used a magnificent word to describe a piddling reality.

I became a member of the infirmary staff. How I happened to be chosen was another story. A short time after my arrival I plucked up my courage to ask Dr. Klein, the chief S.S. doctor of the camp, to allow me to do something to relieve the sufferings of my companions. He rebuked me sharply, for it was forbidden to address an S.S. doctor without authorization. The next day, however, he sought me out and declared that henceforth I would be in charge of liaison with the doctors of the different barracks. He lost a lot of precious time listening to their reports in the course of his rounds and needed help.

Soon a new order was issued. All internees with any knowledge of medical practice should make themselves known. Many volunteered. As I was not without experience, I was ordered into infirmary work.

Deplorable Conditions

Barrack No. 15, probably the most dilapidated in the camp, was to house the new service. The rain leaked through the roof and the walls had enormous, gaping holes. To the right and to the left of the entrance were two small rooms. One was designated the "infirmary" and the other the "pharmacy." A few weeks later, a "hospital" was installed at the other end of the barrack, and we were able to assemble four or five hundred patients.

For a long time, however, we had only the two small rooms. The only light came from the corridor; there was no running water, and the wooden floor was difficult to keep clean, though we washed it twice a day with cold water. Without boiling water and disinfectants, we could not scrub away the traces of blood and pus in the crevices.

The furniture of our infirmary consisted of a pharmacy closet without shelves, a shaky examination table which we had to prop up with bricks, and a long table which we covered with a sheet to hold our instruments. We had little else, and whatever we did have was in poor condition.

Whenever we had to use anything we were confronted with the same problem: should we use the unsterilized instruments or do without them? For example, after treating a boil or an anthrax, we might have to treat an abscess of lesser gravity with the same instruments. We knew that we were exposing our patient to infection. What could we do? It was a miracle that we never had a serious infection because of this situation. Sometimes we wondered whether our experience did not refute all medical theories on sterilization.

Swamped with Work

The internees in our camp totaled from thirty to forty thousand. And the entire personnel in our infirmary consisted of five women! Needless to say, we were swamped with work.

We rose at four in the morning. The consultations began at five. The sick, of whom there were often as many as fifteen hundred in a day, had to wait their turns by rows of five. It was pitiful to behold these columns of ailing women, scantily clad, standing humbly in the rain, snow, or frost. Often when their last strength ebbed they fainted like so many tenpins falling.

The consultations continued without a respite from daybreak until three in the afternoon, when we paused for our rest period. We devoted this time to our soup, if there was any left; and to clean up the floor and the instruments. We operated as late as eight in the evening. Sometimes we had accouchements during the night. We were literally crushed by the burden of the work. Confined to the one hut, which was completely without fresh air, without exercise, and sufficient rest we could not look forward to any relief.

Although we lacked everything, even bandages, we proceeded with fervor, spurred on by our consciousness of the great responsibility. When we felt we were at the end of our resistance we sprinkled our faces and necks with a few drops of precious water. We had to sacrifice these few drops to keep going. But the never-ending effort exhausted us. When there were several accouchements in succession and we had to spend sleepless nights, we became so fatigued that we staggered about as though intoxicated. However, we had an infirmary; and we were doing good, useful work. . . .

Suffering Patients

The result achieved at our infirmary were far from brilliant. The deplorable conditions in the camp caused the number of sick to increase. However, our masters would not augment our personnel. Five women were enough. We could have given part of our medicaments and bandages to the doctors residing in the other barracks, but the Germans would not allow us to do that.

Naturally, we could not take care of all the patients; and many cases were aggravated through neglect; for example, when we had to care for gangrenous wounds. The infections gave off a putrid odor and maggots multiplied rapidly in them. We used a tremendous syringe and disinfected them with a solution of potassium permanganate. But we had to repeat the operation ten or twelve times and our water was exhausted. So as a result, other patients, still waiting, suffered.

The situation eased somewhat when the hospital was installed at the other end of the barrack. This space was reserved for cases requiring surgery, but, in a pinch, all kinds of infections were treated. The hospital held from four to five hundred patients, and was always filled. Moreover, it was difficult to gain admission, so those who were ill frequently had to wait days before being hospitalized. Upon their arrival here, they had to abandon all their effects in exchange for a worthless shirt. They still had to sleep in koias on scanty straw mattresses but with only one blanket for four people. Of course, there could be no question of real scientific isolation.

Selection

Still, the most tragic danger for the sick was the menace of the "selection," which threatened them more than it did the internees in good health. The selection meant a trip to the gas chamber or an injection of phenol in the heart. I first learned about the phenol from Dr. Pasche, an underground member. When the Germans launched their mass selections, it was dangerous to be in the hospital. We therefore encouraged those who were not too ill to stay in their barracks. But, especially in the beginning, the internees refused to believe that hospitalization might be used against them to expedite their journey to the gas chamber. They imagined, naïvely, that the choices made at the hospital and at the roll calls were for transfers to other camps, and that the sick were sent to a central hospital.

Before the infirmary was established and I was assigned to the service of Dr. Klein, I one day told my fellow internees that they should avoid even the appearance of illness. Later that same day I had to accompany Dr. Klein on his rounds. This man was different from the other S.S. He never shouted, and had rather nice manners. One of the sick remarked to him, "We appreciate your kindness, Herr Oberarzt," and she went on to say that some people in the camp pretended that the sick were sent to the gas chamber.

Dr. Klein simulated surprise. With a smile he said, "You don't have to believe all the silly things they say around here. Who spread this rumor?"

I trembled. Only this morning I had told this poor creature the truth. Fortunately, the blocova came to my rescue. She wrinkled her eyebrows and literally crushed the prattler with an icy stare.

The sick woman understood that she had spoken out of turn and beat a hasty retreat. "Oh, I don't know anything about it," she mumbled. "They say all sorts of things around here."

Contagious Diseases

In another camp hospital, Section B-3, there were about six thousand deportees in August, 1944, considerably fewer than our thirty-five thousand. There they had isolated rooms for the contagious cases. Characteristic of the irrational way in which the camps were organized, this, the smaller section, had an infirmary ten times as large as ours, with fifteen doctors on service. However, the hygienic conditions there were even more deplorable, for there were no latrines at all, only wooden chests in the open air, where the female inmates were under the eyes of the S.S. and the male deportees.

Whenever we had contagious cases we had to take them to that section hospital. This troubled us. If we kept the contagious cases, we risked spreading the disease. But once they were in the hospital the sick women ran the risk of being selected. Yet the rule was strict, and we exposed ourselves to dangerous punishment if we kept the contagious cases. Besides, Dr. Mengele made frequent tours and checked up. Needless to say, we infringed upon the rules as often as possible.

The transfer of the contagious cases made a pitiful spectacle as, burning with fever and covered with their blankets, they walked along the "Lagerstrasse." The other inmates avoided them as though they were lepers. Some of the unfortunates were confined in the "Durchgangszimmer" (passageway), a room nine by twelve feet, where the sick had to lie on the bare ground. This was a real antechamber of death.

Those who entered this gateway to destruction were at once removed from the lists of effectives and were thenceforth given nothing to eat. So they had only the final journey to look forward to. At last the "Red Cross" trucks would come and the sick would be packed into them like sardines. Protests were useless. They were piled one on top of another. The German responsible for the shipment locked the door and took his place beside the driver. The truck started its trip to the gas chamber. That was why we dreaded taking contagious cases to the "hospital."

Confusing and Illogical

The system of administration was completely without logic. It was stupefying to see how little the orders which followed one another had in common. This was only partly due to negligence. The Germans apparently sought also to baffle the internees, thus minimizing the danger of revolt. The same methods prevailed with the selections. For a while one category of sick would automatically be selected. Then one day it would all change, and those who had the same affliction, say diphtheria, would be put under treatment in an isolated room under the care of deportee doctors.

Most of the time it was hazardous to have scarlet fever; yet, occasionally, those who had this disease were taken care of, and some were even cured. They were sent back to their old barracks, and their example convinced the others that scarlet fever could not condemn one to the gas chamber. Soon, thereafter, the policy would change again. How could any one know what, therefore, to believe?

Be that as it may, only in very rare cases did our sick ever return from the section hospital, and these had never moved through the Durchgangszimmer, so that they were not well informed of the conditions. That "hospital" remained a horror for all of us. It was surrounded by mystery and filled with danger and death.

Chapter 3

Survival and Daily Life

Chapter Preface

New arrivals at the concentration camps quickly learned that to survive they had to find more food than what they were given: bread made with sawdust; thin, watery soup; and a brown liquid called coffee. Those who could not find other sources of food soon died of starvation. Desperate prisoners frequently stole food from each other, an act that was not punished by the guards. If inmates were caught stealing food from the camps' kitchens—even potato peels found in the garbage—or were found smuggling in food from outside the camp, they were executed by the Nazis.

Adding to the stress of starvation was the inadequate clothing the prisoners were given to wear. New arrivals at the concentration camps were forced to surrender all of their personal belongings, including socks, underwear, and shoes, if they were in good condition. In return, most inmates received a uniform of a striped dress or pants and shirt, a cap, and old shoes. If the supply of uniforms was low, however, the new inmates were given clothing from people who had been gassed or executed, with little regard for whether the clothes would fit or were appropriate for the season. Some prisoners wore woolen Russian army uniforms in the summer; others were given silk ball gowns in the winter.

Shoes were an extremely valuable commodity in the camp; those whose shoes had worn out were given wooden clogs that were difficult to walk in and frequently caused painful blisters and festering sores. Often, the prisoners' feet swelled up so much that they were no longer able to put on their shoes and were forced to go barefoot, even in winter. Wearing clogs or going shoeless in the winter made it more difficult for prisoners to keep up when marching in formation, and if they could not keep up, they were beaten by the guards, executed on the spot, or selected for the gas chambers.

Roll Call

Max Mayr

> Roll call—also known as *appell*—in the concentration camp
> was a ritual that was feared and dreaded by the inmates. Max
> Mayr, a prisoner at the concentration camp at Buchenwald,
> provides the following eyewitness account of roll calls at the
> camp. Roll call was held several times during the day: in the
> morning before work, after work, before bed, whenever there
> was to be a selection, whenever there was an escape, or for a
> multitude of any other reasons. He explains how the stated
> purpose of a roll call was to count the prisoners to determine
> if any were missing. If the number of prisoners present did
> not tally with the number of prisoners listed, the entire camp
> was made to stand at attention until the numbers matched. In-
> mates were also made to stand at attention for roll no matter
> the weather—broiling sun, pouring rain, subzero tempera-
> tures. In this regard, the Nazis used roll call as a form of tor-
> ture. There was no excuse for missing a roll call; even the
> dead were dragged out to be counted.

The roll calls that took place daily were feared by all
prisoners, especially in the early years. Often one had
to stand for hours in the icy cold or in stormy weather, after a hard day's work. But the SS wanted to count their slave
workers precisely every day, as many of them of course har-
bored thoughts of escape and often enough even attempted
to flee—which always meant retaliation against the entire
camp.

Of course the statistics for roll call had to be prepared by
prisoners because no SS man could ever have carried out

Excerpted from *The Buchenwald Report*, translated and edited by David A. Hackett. Copyright © 1995 by Westview Press, a member of the Perseus Books Group. Reprinted by
permission of Westview Press, a member of Perseus Books LLC.

these painfully exact mathematical calculations. We constantly strove to avoid mistakes in setting up the lists because searching them out during roll call would have unnecessarily prolonged the process and robbed exhausted comrades of their free time. This meant special care in

Punishment

No inmate in any German concentration camp during World War II could ever hope to escape punishment. From the moment prisoners arrived at the camp, they could expect to be hit and beaten for the most minor of offenses. Even if a prisoner was not personally guilty of a transgression, he or she would be punished collectively for the sins of others. The authors of the following excerpt were Polish political prisoners who describe some of the punishments meted out by the Germans at Auschwitz.

For breaking camp rules, slowness at work, lack of energy at drill, talking at work, or else a reckless loud word on the Block, the prisoners were punished immediately with beatings by the SS men, *Blockführers,* Kapos, or group leaders, or else reported to the camp Kommandant. The beatings varied: a blow to the face with a fist; a kick in the stomach or groin; a strike with a switch across the back; but also crushing blows with a pole; the knocking out of teeth; the breaking of ribs; the cracking open of heads. Some trained themselves to beat so that they could kill a man with a single blow.

At the Appel [roll call], obviously, to explain yourself without authority, or to present your case, led either to corporal punishment (from ten to a hundred lashes, administered by the ordinary SS or one of the officers), or to punishment on the stake. That punishment consisted of tying the hands of the condemned behind his back and hanging him with handcuffs to a gallows. The best-exercised man might endure this position for a few minutes, after which counting the numerous service detail prisoners, who because of their work were not required to appear at roll call.

It is clear that with a camp population of 5,000 to 7,000, a missing person is rather quickly noticed. It is different with 35,000; because of the overcrowding of the blocks, a

---

the muscles weakened and the shoulders, dislocated from their sockets, slowly turned above the head. The tortured man fainted, of course; he was then lowered, water was poured over him, and he was beaten until he regained consciousness, and, then, he was hanged again. The third punishment, was to be sent to the *SK,* the penal company, where there was particular rigor; the *Blockführer* and the Kapo were specially chosen, and the work correspondingly arduous, often lasted longer than in the rest of the camp. At the beginning of Auschwitz, the life of a man in the penal company did not last longer than one month. They say that there was a custom in the first years of the penal company of hanging a noose in the doors of the Block after the evening Appel, and prisoners voluntarily hanged themselves while the whole Block sang in chorus, *"Góralu, czy ci nie zal—* Moutaineer, aren't you sorry?" There was always a crowd by the noose.

The punishment preliminary to the penal company, other than beating, was the so-called bunker, a cement cage 30cm × 50cm × 200cm in which the prisoners were locked—whether after work for one night, or continuously for several months—and spent the whole time in one position without moving.

There was no gradation of crime. Hanging for a loaf of bread and for attempted escape; punishment with the bunker for diamonds and for collusion with the SS men; the *SK* was given for a piece of worn blanket used to wrap the feet, or for lighting a cigarette during work.

Janusz Nel Siedleck, Krystyn Olszewski, and Tadeusz Borowski, *We Were in Auschwitz.* New York: Welcome Rain, 2000.

precise check was almost impossible. In addition, many foreign prisoners thought of roll call as a Prussian drill that one should simply avoid. They unfortunately gave no thought to the fact that by doing so they endangered the free time of tens of thousands. For if a single person was missing, often 800 numbers and names had to be called, usually with the help of interpreters. One can imagine how long that took, especially when furious SS men struck prisoners and shouted at them during the process. Thus in the final years roll call was never completed in less than an hour and a half.

Horrible Tragedies

Roll call square saw many horrible tragedies. How often, when a prisoner had escaped, did the entire camp have to remain standing! Twice, in 1938 and 1939, the camp had to stand for eighteen or nineteen hours straight, costing many people their lives. We were often frisked in roll call square; that is, we had to empty our pockets, and the SS inspected the contents, during which a great deal of money and tobacco disappeared. One time we had to undress completely and stand naked for two hours while we were frisked. All executions until the end of 1942 took place in roll call square. The whipping block in particular was put to use at almost every roll call.

At the same time roll call accomplished its function in the Nazi annihilation plan against antifascists. Many met their deaths after hard hours of standing in the square. In the famine of winter 1939, when the horrible grub led to a dysentery and typhus epidemic, hundreds literally fell: The square was covered with the dead and dying at every roll call. Anyone who had died in the block or work detail during the day had to be dragged to the square. In many blocks sixty to seventy lay dead and dying. Gypsies in particular died like flies during this winter. Only a few out of several hundred were still living by summer. Yet even in "normal" times the dead and murdered comrades lay alongside their blocks for a final roll call, for the SS insisted on "order" down to a prisoner's last breath. Only after roll call were the dying allowed into the hospital; the murdered were taken to the morgue.

Great Confusion

When the great evacuation transports came out of the east, an orderly roll call was no longer possible. SS sentries only hastily counted the half-starved figures who staggered through the gate, so an exact determination of the number of prisoners in the camp was no longer possible. Moreover, of course, there were no transport lists—which would have been inaccurate anyway, as on every transport many comrades escaped and still more died and were thrown out of the train. The confusion during roll call was so great that, on one evening, for example, the books would show three prisoners missing, but by the following evening there would be seventeen too many, even though no new transport had arrived. Roll call had by then lost all meaning even for the SS.

After April 3, 1945, therefore, no more roll calls were held under SS command. At that time there were 80,900 in the Buchenwald camp system, of which 45,000 were in external details and about 36,000 in the base camp. Through continuous arrivals from subsidiary camps, the number in Buchenwald itself rose very rapidly to 48,000. Then began the evacuation of the camp, which went on until 21,400 comrades remained. These comrades then took part in the first "freedom roll call" on April 12, 1945.

Starvation

Livia Bitton-Jackson

> A stated purpose of the concentration camps was to work Jews
> to death. As a part of this strategy, the Nazis fed the inmates
> starvation rations. Inmates typically received a hot liquid that
> was called coffee in the morning, a liter of thin, watery soup
> for lunch, and a slice of bread made with sawdust for dinner,
> occasionally accompanied by a small amount of margarine,
> lard, or jelly. This meager diet was all inmates could expect to
> receive unless they managed to find an illegal source of food
> in the camp. However, prisoners found with contraband food
> were severely punished and sometimes even executed. Despite
> the threat of death, starving prisoners eagerly devoured any
> food they could find, whether it was potato peelings or rotten,
> spoiled beets found in the garbage, or fresh blades of grass
> growing in the camp. In the following essay, Livia Bitton-
> Jackson, who was in Auschwitz with her mother, describes
> how some people who are starving can overcome feelings of
> squeamishness and eat food that others cannot.

The brief morning *Zählappel* [roll call] is followed by a
work lineup of thousands of inmates. The dreaded *Kapos* arrive, and each *Kapo* selects several hundred workers
for his commando from among us.

The word *Kapo* means supreme authority over life and
death. Delegated absolute power by the SS, the *Kapos* of
Plaszow, as if they had made a pact with the devil, exercise
all methods of control—brutal beatings and torture to
death—with relish. They seem to rise above the need for human response, or contact, even among each other.

From *I Have Lived a Thousand Years: Growing Up in the Holocaust*, by Livia Bitton-
Jackson. Copyright © 1997 Livia Bitton-Jackson. Reprinted with the permission of
Simon & Schuster Books for Young Readers, an imprint of Simon & Schuster Children's
Publishing Division.

I observe with dread the awesome figure of our *Kapo* standing high on a rock or boulder, whip in hand. Several younger assistants snap to his command. If you stop to rest for a moment, the *Kapo* instantly dispatches one of his boys and the lash whips you back to your routine. Were the lad's strikes tempered with a touch of compassion, the *Kapo* would admonish from his high perch:

"At her head, *Liebling!* Are you losing touch? Let her have it in the head!"

If you cried out in pain, the lashings would double. In time we learned to stifle even our whimpers. In time we learned to endure in silence.

Our work consists of *Planierung,* straightening the hilltop with spades and shovels in preparation for construction. The work was very difficult in the beginning. When we first arrived in the hills, we were exhausted from the mountain climbing alone. And that, at the start of a twelve-hour workday.

Now that we've become somewhat acclimatized, the work is much more bearable. The bruises on our hands have turned into callouses. Our backs got used to bending without pain. Digging, shoveling, and wheelbarrowing became endurable. If only we could stop to rest for a few moments from time to time!

Yesterday an older woman a few feet from me stopped to rest her arms. Instead of taking the trouble of administering the whip, the young assistant picked up a piece of rock and slung it at her. The rock slashed a deep, bloody gap in the elderly lady's head, and she collapsed unconscious. The boy, taken aback, ran over to the stricken inmate, then turned apologetically to his master. The *Kapo* admonished with a devilish chuckle, "You missed, you stupid *Junge!* She's only fainted. You should've struck her dead!"

The Noon Meal

At noon we have half an hour rest when we receive our cooked meal. It's a bowlful of pottage, or cabbage soup with grain.

This morning the food arrived early. As it stood for hours in the sun, it became putrefied and alive with worms. I noticed a long, white worm wiggling in Mommy's spoon as she lifted it to her mouth. I shrieked with horror. Mommy was startled; she looked at me with astonishment. "What happened?"

"Mommy, there's a worm on your spoon! Look, Mommy, there are hundreds of worms in your bowl! And in mine! Look!"

"Nonsense! These are not worms. Eat, and leave me alone."

"But Mommy, these are worms. Live worms. They crawl. Look."

I pick one of the swarming insects out of my bowl and place it on the ground. It begins crawling. Then I pick another. It, too, begins crawling.

Mommy looks at me with helpless despair. "What are you trying to do? What is your objective? Tell me, what do you want of me?"

I do not understand. I wanted to save Mommy from a horrible fate: disease, or death. Or simply from the horror of swallowing worms. Instead, she is furious with me. My mother, the finicky lady who had been reluctant to eat in restaurants, and even in friends' houses, for fear the vegetables, or hands, were not washed thoroughly enough; who baked, not only cookies and cakes, but even our daily bread at home, for fear the flour in bakery goods had not been carefully sifted, now is glaring at me.

"I can't leave this food. I am very hungry. Do you want me to die of hunger?" Her voice is beyond recognition. Her facial expression is beyond recognition as she goes on, "And there are no worms in it! Say no more of it!"

As Mommy continues eating I turn my bowl over, spilling its contents on the ground, and run. I sit on a boulder at a distance, and begin to cry. My God. My dear God, is this actually happening?

Underground Commerce

Samuel Willenberg

When prisoners arrived at the concentration camps, many were bringing their most valuable possessions with them for they were often told, and in fact, encouraged, by the Nazis to bring whatever they would need with them. However, the prisoners soon learned this encouragement was a cruel trick as they were forced to give up everything they owned, including the clothes on their back, at the camp. In this way Germany obtained untold wealth, for all the possessions were eventually sent to Berlin. The clothing was distributed among needy Germans, while the rest of the plunder ended up in the state's coffers.

A special work detail was needed to sort through all the new arrivals' belongings. This was a highly coveted *kommando,* as the workers were permitted to keep the food they found. Although they were required to turn over all the other valuables, many risked severe punishment or death by smuggling money, gold, diamonds, medicines, and other contraband back into camp. Once in the camp, the smuggled items could be given away or traded for favors, food, clothing, and other vital goods. Thus, the belongings of the new arrivals were responsible for a flourishing underground market in the camps.

In the following essay, Samuel Willenberg describes other aspects of the underground economy in the camps. Willenberg, who had worked in the sorting *kommando,* was transferred to a new job working outside the camp where the

Excerpted from *Surviving Treblinka*, by Samuel Willenberg (New York: Basil Blackwell, 1989). Copyright © 1989 Samuel Willenberg. Reprinted by permission of the publisher.

workers were guarded by Ukrainian soldiers instead of the customary SS officers. The arrangement benefited both sides, he asserts; the Ukrainians, who sold the inmates food and liquor, were able to finance their trips to the local brothel, while the workers were able to provide necessities for themselves and their fellow prisoners.

The day after we moved huts, the Germans ordered the 'Reds' [political prisoners] to dig up the ground in the hut where we had previously lived. They suspected us of having buried valuables there. SS men supervised the prisoners as they worked. Jewellery and gold—about 50 kilograms in all—were discovered. We were terribly embarrassed.

Contraband and Punishment

The reaction came swiftly. During roll call we were informed that each of us would undergo a personal body search, and that anyone who wanted to avoid trouble would immediately return all silver, gold, watches, rings and documents in his possession. Among the prisoners, only foremen and *Kapos* were allowed to possess watches. I was one of the few who had no valuables to return. As the announcement was made, Fessele of the SS stood behind us and monitored our reactions. Suddenly he spotted a few gold coins at the feet of one of the prisoners. He pounced on the offender, shoved him into the barbed wire and, his head against the wire, punched him. Then he ordered us to stand beside the hut. Now Fessele began to circulate among us, and ordered each rank of five to pass before him. Now and then he singled out specific prisoners for body search. Suddenly I recalled that I had a false 'Aryan' birth certificate which I had kept in case of an escape from Treblinka. Such a document, at this time, could prove my undoing; it would be hard to rid myself of it while standing in rank. So, without giving the matter great thought, I shredded it in my pocket, and, carefully, stuffed it into my mouth, chewed it up with no perceptible motion, and swallowed. The Protestant minister, standing beside me, thought I was eating. I laughed and passed him a bit of paper. He looked at me angrily, thinking I was unwilling to share my delicacies and that I was mocking him; he stopped talking to me. Only that evening was I able to explain what had really happened.

Though Fessele continued to search the prisoners in the meantime, he found nothing apart from some scattered coins whose owner would not confess. As we watched, Fessele pulled the two prisoners closest to the gold coins out of line and shot them, together with the first man he had apprehended.

A prisoner of the 'potato detail', too, was murdered that day. This group was in charge of dealing with mountains of potatoes and turnips. For having been caught cooking some potatoes, he was beaten viciously, made to stand for a whole day with his hands up, and then shot. This was not an isolated case in Treblinka; prisoners were frequently killed for taking potatoes while at work.

A New Work Detail

At about this time Galewski pulled me out of the clothes-sorting detail and reassigned me to the *Tarnungskommando,* a group with the rather easy task of camouflaging the camp from the inside against outside observers. I had hungered for such an assignment and was grateful to Galewski, who had interceded with Sidow of the SS to get me the position. The reason I was so pleased was that the work involved leaving the camp and entering the forest. Even then, I was thinking about a break-out.

Our detail comprised fifteen men, whose job it was to dig holes, slip tree trunks into them, and stretch barbed wire between them. Once the wire was in place, we filled the spaces with pine branches, which we procured in the nearby forest, tied into bundles, and lugged to the camp.

Like the other work details, we lined up every day at

6 A.M., after roll call. Sidow came up to us. Seeing me in the group for the first time, he sized me up from all angles, like a farmer with a new horse, and pronounced me fit for the job. Sidow was short, and the high-cut boots he always wore made him look even shorter. He wore a cap with a skull emblem; his face was round, his nose red and creased, and one could immediately identify him as an alcoholic. He had a little black Hitler moustache. His full lips were poised crookedly, and he worked very hard at looking cruel. He manipulated his whip like an orchestra conductor and pounded it against his boots. Aware of his stumpy stature, he not only wore high-heeled boots but also tried at all times to walk on tiptoe, so as to make himself look taller.

We stood beside the hut as our foreman, Kleinbaum, approached Sidow, reported the number of workers, and added a few compliments about his appearance. Sidow ached for compliments, and Kleinbaum did not spare any. Now six armed Ukrainians in black uniforms came over. They balanced on one leg, and, looking at us all the while, perched their rifle butts on their raised knees to load them bullet by bullet. Then they surrounded us and took aim. With a crack of his whip, Sidow ordered us forward. Off we went, toward the camp gate and into the forest. To the left we passed two SS huts, spanking clean and ringed by flowerbeds. To the right was the infirmary reserved for SS men and Ukrainians. At its door stood Dr Chorążycki, who smiled at us. The SS officer on duty (his dogtag announcing his position) stopped us at the gate opening into the forest. After counting us, he ordered the Ukrainians on duty with him to open the gate, a country-style affair built by Wiernik of the *Todeslager* [death camp]. Outside the entrance stood a sign in German: '*SS Sonderkommando Treblinka, Distrikt Warsaw*'.

Into the Forest

We were outside Treblinka. The forest immediately took over, and there, with Ukrainians on all sides, we worked. Stepping away from the group was strictly forbidden. We worked next to one another and, by order of Sidow and the Ukrainians, sang aloud. When we had gone about a kilometre from the camp, Sidow decided he had found a good place to start chopping branches. A good place, to him, was an isolated one where the forest was not too dense, so his Ukrainians could watch over us. We climbed nearby trees, sometimes in pairs. The Ukrainians followed our every movement, rifles trained. We threw the cut branches to the ground; once enough had been accumulated, we jumped from the trees and tied the branches into bundles with some belts, the legacy of murdered Jews, that we had brought from the sorting-yard for this purpose.

We tried to keep the piles as light as possible, of course; we were not strong enough for heavy hauling, and wanted another opportunity to leave the camp. Sidow examined the bundles with the opposite intention. When he felt the bundles were too light, he sometimes forced us to add to them. Only after rechecking and reweighing them did he let us sit down. From that moment we were not to stand up; we could only move about in a very small area beside the bundles, and then only on our knees. This stricture applied also to *Vorarbeiter* [foreman] Kleinbaum. Then, without shame, Sidow opened his fly. He turned his back to us, took a few steps and, with his stumpy, taut body, strained to urinate.

The Trade

The Ukrainians, rifles aimed, surrounded us throughout. Now one of them flipped us a skull-emblem cap and said in Russian, 'So, comrades: give money!' Each of us gave what he had. Dollars, gold coins and gold roubles stamped with the head of the Tsar spilled out. Kleinbaum asked the guard what kind of package we would get in return. If its contents would just suffice for lunch, Kleinbaum would pay $300–400. Hearing the offer, the guard, like a typical beggar, took the money which Kleinbaum pulled out of the cap and walked toward the railway. The package proved to contain a 4-kilogram loaf of dark village bread, a litre of vodka,

3 kilos of bacon, a few cans of sardines and some chocolate. The amount of money involved was a Rockefeller fortune in Poland at the time. We divided the victuals equally, irrespective of each prisoner's contribution, if any (not everyone had foreign currency), and downed the food on the spot. Now it was time for personal business. For $100—or $20 in gold—the guard provided us with parcels which we might take back to the camp. Such a package usually contained half a litre of vodka, a kilo of bacon and a loaf of bread. We concealed the treasure in the bundles of pine branches and under our shirts, where our sunken bellies left ample room. I was particularly well qualified for this, because I had become so skinny that a loaf of bread hardly showed.

High Spirits

Just as we had hidden our booty and got ourselves ready to return to the camp, Sidow materialized. In one hand he carried a half-litre of vodka which the guards had given him, and in the other a slab of bacon. He approached several of us and stuck the bottle under our noses. We sucked the vodka into our throats without letting our lips touch it. We sat and drank, the bottle going from hand to hand. Suddenly Sidow turned to me. 'Katzap, come here. Crawl!' I obeyed. As I reached him, he sat down on my back and, like a disturbed child, brought his whip down on me and shouted, 'Faster, faster!' He imagined a famous master horseman astride a wild pony. The steed, to my distress, was me. I circled the seated group of prisoners with my rider, to the applause of the Ukrainians and the foreman. Suddenly I slipped and crashed to the ground; my intrepid equestrian tumbled through the air and landed flat beside me, arms outstretched and stubby legs splayed on either side. I burst into laughter, as did Sidow. We rested on a moist, green patch of earth with dense pines overhead. For a moment we forgot our situation. Then came a shout: 'Up! Back to the camp'. We gathered the bundles of branches, loaded them onto our backs and marched toward the camp, watchful Ukrainians all around. Sidow tottered drunkenly, issuing confused orders. The Ukrainians, rifles trained, were sober despite the booze they had imbibed; they led us to the camp. Their spirits were good, for they had earned great quantities of gold and dollars from our dealings. Now they could afford to cavort with whores in the neighbouring villages—sluts whom the peasants had brought from Warsaw specially for them.

Back at the Camp

As the Ukrainian on duty at the camp gate admitted us, we headed toward the guardroom and saw Lalka of the SS standing at the porch. He hopped down the stairs and slowly approached Sidow. Hands on chest Napoleon-style, he looked us over smirkingly. From a distance we saw Sidow gesturing in our direction and muttering something in his alcoholic daze. Whatever it was, Lalka reacted by giving him a ringing smack in the face. Then he shouted at us 'Out to work!'

Buckling under the pine branches, we marched unchecked into the camp. Once we had passed through the gate, the Ukrainians returned to their huts and we went to the fence to insert the branches. Our comrades came up to us as we worked and unloaded the food we had procured. Alfred approached me with his ever-present pram. Meant in fact to assist him in collecting rubbish, it allowed him free movement throughout the camp. When asked if I had brought anything for him and his friends, I reached into his pile of rags and, bending to slip branches into the bottom of the fence, slipped into the rags the package hidden under the pine branches, and the bread concealed in the cavity of my stomach.

In general, we visited the forest several times a month. The determining factors were the need for wood in the camp, or for camouflage. Though we always returned with food, they never searched us. Even Miete, who substituted for Sidow when the little SS man was on leave in Germany, tolerated our speculation. Other prisoners who for some reason or another were sent into the forest were scrupulously searched, and anyone caught with food or vodka was hauled to the *Lazarett*[1] for a bullet in the head. We wondered why a *Tarnungskommando* was given such privileged treatment, and concluded that it was meant to dissuade us from trying to escape. . . .

Underground Commerce

'Underground' was an unfamiliar word in the camp, for each and every prisoner, was an underground unto himself. An asset such as a slice of sausage was 'underground' property in a way, for to be found with it spelled an SS bullet in the head. The hunger which had dominated the camp for the past six months, and the awareness that one might not survive another day, caused prisoners to live for the moment alone, without thinking of the morrow. At risk of our lives we would slip out at night and buy packages of food from the Ukrainians, paying for them in dollars and gold. All this commerce went on through two open windows in the outhouse between the two halls of the first hut. The idea was that, if by chance the Germans discovered what was going on, they would not punish the prisoners in the halls and would not suspect that the traders were the prisoners who slept on either side of the windows. In order to buy a package, the prisoner would stick his hand through the outhouse window and pass his money to the Ukrainian standing outside.

The SS men tried to put an end to the nocturnal smuggling. They stood outside the window and, imitating the Ukrainians, murmured *'Paczka'*—Polish for 'package'. When a hand clutching money appeared through the window, the SS man would slice it with his knife. At morning role call they would inspect us for casualties and, having

---

1. A building masquerading as a hospital. The old, young, and infirm were sent there to be shot and cremated.

identified the delinquent, would send him to his death in the *Lazarett.*

The Paradox

The paradox of all this was that, unless someone tried to approach the outer fence, the Ukrainians who guarded us were not allowed to shoot or beat us without an order from the Germans, lest they try to extort money from prisoners by beating them. The Germans knew we found money and valuables while sorting the clothing of dead Jews, and did not want the Ukrainians to lay their hands on the treasure— because it was all supposed to go to Germany. The Ukrainian who guarded us knew that, as long as we lived, he had someone from whom to extort money for his carousing and boozing in the neighbouring villages. Though the Ukrainians who were caught at this commerce did not face death by shooting as we did, they were punished severely for their offence. They did not hesitate to run the risk anyway, because they received tremendous sums of money in return for a few parcels of food. Supplies of this kind therefore reached the camp each night. During the typhus epidemic, we even 'ordered' oranges and lemons for our patients. Enough money could procure anything. Thus, though it claimed many victims, trade with the Ukrainian guards persisted for the duration.

Apathy

Viktor E. Frankl

Viktor E. Frankl was a Jewish psychiatrist who was sent to
Auschwitz in 1944. The following essay is an excerpt from
his book *Man's Search for Meaning,* in which he explains his
theory of logotherapy. According to Frankl, logotherapy
stresses people's ability to rise above their suffering and discover the meaning of their life, regardless of the circumstances in which they find themselves. Frankl developed this
theory during his year in Auschwitz when he discovered that
inmates went through distinct phases in the acceptance of
their condition. Like other prisoners, Frankl was initially horrified and shamed by his circumstances; however, he gradually learned that in order to survive, he must deaden his feelings toward the inhumanity and cruelty that existed in the
camp. Apathy—the feeling of not caring anymore—was vital
in forming a necessary shell to protect himself against the
atrocities he saw and experienced. When his emotions toward
others were blunted, then he could focus all his energy on
saving himself.

I think it was [German dramatist and critic Gotthold] Less-
ing who once said, "There are things which must cause
you to lose your reason or you have none to lose." An abnormal reaction to an abnormal situation is normal behavior. Even we psychiatrists expect the reactions of a man to
an abnormal situation, such as being committed to an asy-
lum, to be abnormal in proportion to the degree of his nor-
mality. The reaction of a man to his admission to a concentration camp also represents an abnormal state of mind, but

judged objectively it is a normal and . . . typical reaction to the given circumstances. These reactions . . . began to change in a few days. The prisoner passed from the first [phase, i.e. shock] to the second phase; the phase of relative apathy in which he achieved a kind of emotional death. . . .

Painful Emotions

The newly arrived prisoner experienced the tortures of other most painful emotions, all of which he tried to deaden. First of all, there was his boundless longing for his home and his family. This often could become so acute that he felt himself consumed by longing. Then there was disgust; disgust with all the ugliness which surrounded him, even in its mere external forms.

Most of the prisoners were given a uniform of rags which would have made a scarecrow elegant by comparison. Between the huts in the camp lay pure filth, and the more one worked to clear it away, the more one had to come in contact with it. It was a favorite practice to detail a new arrival to a work group whose job was to clean the latrines and remove the sewage. If, as usually happened, some of the excrement splashed into his face during its transport over bumpy fields, any sign of disgust by the prisoner or any attempt to wipe off the filth would only be punished with a blow from a Capo. And thus the mortification of normal reactions was hastened.

At first the prisoner looked away if he saw the punishment parades of another group; he could not bear to see fellow prisoners march up and down for hours in the mire, their movements directed by blows. Days or weeks later things changed. Early in the morning, when it was still dark, the prisoner stood in front of the gate with his detachment, ready to march. He heard a scream and saw how a comrade was knocked down, pulled to his feet again, and knocked down once more—and why? He was feverish but had reported to sick-bay at an improper time. He was being punished for this irregular attempt to be relieved of his duties.

Blunted Feelings

But the prisoner who had passed into the second stage of his psychological reactions did not avert his eyes any more. By then his feelings were blunted, and he watched unmoved. Another example: he found himself waiting at sick-bay, hoping to be granted two days of light work inside the camp because of injuries or perhaps edema or fever. He stood unmoved while a twelve-year-old boy was carried in who had been forced to stand at attention for hours in the snow or to work outside with bare feet because there were no shoes for him in the camp. His toes had become frostbitten, and the doctor on duty picked off the black gangrenous stumps with tweezers, one by one. Disgust, horror and pity are emotions that our spectator could not really feel any more. The sufferers, the dying and the dead, became such commonplace sights to him after a few weeks of camp life that they could not move him any more.

I spent some time in a hut for typhus patients who ran very high temperatures and were often delirious, many of them moribund. After one of them had just died, I watched without any emotional upset the scene that followed, which was repeated over and over again with each death. One by one the prisoners approached the still warm body. One grabbed the remains of a messy meal of potatoes; another decided that the corpse's wooden shoes were an improvement on his own, and exchanged them. A third man did the same with the dead man's coat, and another was glad to be able to secure some—just imagine!—genuine string.

All this I watched with unconcern. Eventually I asked the "nurse" to remove the body. When he decided to do so, he took the corpse by its legs, allowing it to drop into the small corridor between the two rows of boards which were the beds for the fifty typhus patients, and dragged it across the bumpy earthen floor toward the door. The two steps which led up into the open air always constituted a problem for us, since we were exhausted from a chronic lack of food. After a few months' stay in the camp we could not walk up those steps, which were each about six inches high, without putting our hands on the door jambs to pull ourselves up.

The man with the corpse approached the steps. Wearily he dragged himself up. Then the body: first the feet, then the trunk, and finally—with an uncanny rattling noise—the head of the corpse bumped up the two steps.

Bread for Shoes

Prisoners in the death camps were forced to give up all their possessions—including the clothes on their backs and the shoes and stockings on their feet—when they arrived in the camps. In exchange, they were given rags to wear and allowed to pick through cast-off shoes for replacements. When these shoes wore out, they were replaced with wooden clogs. Helen Sendyk explains why shoes were so important to the inmates.

After food, clothing was our greatest problem. Our shoes were wearing out from all the marching. Business deals developed, and the going currency was our bread ration. A discarded belt from a factory motor would be concealed and carried back to camp. It might be bartered for three portions of bread. Another portion would buy the services of the prison's shoemaker, who would use the leather belt to resole a pair of worn shoes. Now the girl would have the shoes to save her feet, but it would have cost her stomach four days of bread rations.

Others were not so lucky. Their shoes were gone altogether by now, and the camp provided them with clogs. Those thick wooden soles with cloth uppers offered poor protection for their weary feet. Heavy and abrasive, they made marching a torture. During the summer many prisoners carried the clogs over their shoulders and marched in bare feet, but in freezing winter weather this was impossible.

Helen Sendyk, *The End of Days.* New York: St. Martin's Press, 1992.

My place was on the opposite side of the hut, next to the small, sole window, which was built near the floor. While my cold hands clasped a bowl of hot soup from which I sipped greedily, I happened to look out the window. The corpse which had just been removed stared in at me with glazed eyes. Two hours before I had spoken to that man. Now I continued sipping my soup.

If my lack of emotion had not surprised me from the standpoint of professional interest, I would not remember this incident now, because there was so little feeling involved in it.

A Necessary Protective Shell

Apathy, the blunting of the emotions and the feeling that one could not care any more, were the symptoms arising during the second stage of the prisoner's psychological reactions, and which eventually made him insensitive to daily and hourly beatings. By means of this insensibility the prisoner soon surrounded himself with a very necessary protective shell.

Beatings occurred on the slightest provocation, sometimes for no reason at all. For example, bread was rationed out at our work site and we had to line up for it. Once, the man behind me stood off a little to one side and that lack of symmetry displeased the SS guard. I did not know what was going on in the line behind me, nor in the mind of the SS guard, but suddenly I received two sharp blows on my head. Only then did I spot the guard at my side who was using his stick. At such a moment it is not the physical pain which hurts the most (and this applies to adults as much as to punished children); it is the mental agony caused by the injustice, the unreasonableness of it all.

The Blows That Hurt

Strangely enough, a blow which does not even find its mark can, under certain circumstances, hurt more than one that finds its mark. Once I was standing on a railway track in a snowstorm. In spite of the weather our party had to keep on working. I worked quite hard at mending the track with gravel, since that was the only way to keep warm. For only one moment I paused to get my breath and to lean on my shovel. Unfortunately the guard turned around just then and thought I was loafing. The pain he caused me was not from any insults or any blows. That guard did not think it worth his while to say anything, not even a swear word, to the ragged, emaciated figure standing before him, which probably reminded him only vaguely of a human form. Instead, he playfully picked up a stone and threw it at me. That, to me, seemed the way to attract the attention of a beast, to call a domestic animal back to its job, a creature with which you have so little in common that you do not even punish it.

The most painful part of beatings is the insult which they imply. At one time we had to carry some long, heavy girders over icy tracks. If one man slipped, he endangered not only himself but all the others who carried the same girder. An old friend of mine had a congenitally dislocated hip. He was glad to be capable of working in spite of it, since the physically disabled were almost certainly sent to death when a selection took place. He limped over the track with an especially heavy girder, and seemed about to fall and drag the others with him. As yet, I was not carrying a girder so I jumped to his assistance without stopping to think. I was immediately hit on the back, rudely reprimanded and ordered to return to my place. A few minutes previously the same guard who struck me had told us deprecatingly that we "pigs" lacked the spirit of comradeship.

Indignation

Another time, in a forest, with the temperature at 2° F, we began to dig up the topsoil, which was frozen hard, in order to lay water pipes. By then I had grown rather weak physically. Along came a foreman with chubby rosy cheeks. His face definitely reminded me of a pig's head. I noticed that he wore lovely warm gloves in that bitter cold. For a time he watched me silently. I felt that trouble was brewing, for in front of me lay the mound of earth which showed exactly how much I had dug.

Then he began: "You pig, I have been watching you the whole time! I'll teach you to work, yet! Wait till you dig dirt with your teeth—you'll die like an animal! In two days I'll finish you off! You've never done a stroke of work in your life. What were you, swine? A businessman?"

I was past caring. But I had to take his threat of killing me seriously, so I straightened up and looked him directly in the eye. "I was a doctor—a specialist."

"What? A doctor? I bet you got a lot of money out of people."

"As it happens, I did most of my work for no money at all, in clinics for the poor." But, now, I had said too much. He threw himself on me and knocked me down, shouting like a madman. I can no longer remember what he shouted.

I want to show with this apparently trivial story that there are moments when indignation can rouse even a seemingly hardened prisoner—indignation not about cruelty or pain, but about the insult connected with it. That time blood rushed to my head because I had to listen to a man judge my life who had so little idea of it, a man (I must confess: the following remark, which I made to my fellow-prisoners after the scene, afforded me childish relief) "who looked so vulgar and brutal that the nurse in the out-patient ward in my hospital would not even have admitted him to the waiting room." . . .

Regression

Apathy, the main symptom of the second phase, was a necessary mechanism of self-defense. Reality dimmed, and all efforts and all emotions were centered on one task: preserving one's own life and that of the other fellow. It was typical to hear the prisoners, while they were being herded back to camp from their work sites in the evening, sigh with relief and say, "Well, another day is over."

It can be readily understood that such a state of strain, coupled with the constant necessity of concentrating on the task of staying alive, forced the prisoner's inner life down to a primitive level. Several of my colleagues in camp who were trained in psychoanalysis often spoke of a "regression" in the camp inmate—a retreat to a more primitive form of mental life. His wishes and desires became obvious in his dreams.

What did the prisoner dream about most frequently? Of bread, cake, cigarettes, and nice warm baths. The lack of having these simple desires satisfied led him to seek wish-fulfillment in dreams. Whether these dreams did any good is another matter; the dreamer had to wake from them to the reality of camp life, and to the terrible contrast between that and his dream illusions.

I shall never forget how I was roused one night by the groans of a fellow prisoner, who threw himself about in his sleep, obviously having a horrible nightmare. Since I had always been especially sorry for people who suffered from fearful dreams or deliria, I wanted to wake the poor man. Suddenly I drew back the hand which was ready to shake him, frightened at the thing I was about to do. At that moment I became intensely conscious of the fact that no dream, no matter how horrible, could be as bad as the reality of the camp which surrounded us, and to which I was about to recall him. . . .

A Complete Lack of Sentiment

Undernourishment, besides being the cause of the general preoccupation with food, probably also explains the fact that the sexual urge was generally absent. Apart from the initial effects of shock, this appears to be the only explanation of a phenomenon which a psychologist was bound to observe in those all-male camps: that, as opposed to all other strictly

male establishments—such as army barracks—there was little sexual perversion. Even in his dreams the prisoner did
not seem to concern himself with sex, although his frus-
trated emotions and his finer, higher feelings did find definite expression in them.

With the majority of the prisoners, the primitive life and
the effort of having to concentrate on just saving one's skin
led to a total disregard of anything not serving that purpose,
and explained the prisoners' complete lack of sentiment.

Chapter 4

Confronting Death

Chapter Preface

P risoners were confronted with death even before they arrived at the concentration camps. They were locked in cattle cars for days at a time with no food or water. The very old, the very young, and the sick often died en route to the camps. The passengers were forced to keep the dead bodies with them until the Nazis opened the boxcar doors. Once the prisoners arrived at the camps, they saw their loved ones led off to the gas chambers, never to be seen again. Inside the camps, they were shocked at the emaciated shells of human beings, not realizing that shortly they would become walking skeletons themselves.

The Nazi guards, as well as the *kapos*—the inmates appointed by the guards to be in charge of the barracks and work details—were frequently sadistic and brutal. Prisoners risked deadly beatings for trivial reasons, things such as stumbling while marching, taking too long in the latrine, or taking a break during work. Inmates were forced to watch as the Nazis executed prisoners—innocent and guilty—as retribution for theft, smuggling, sabotage, attempted escape, and other reasons.

The prisoners lived in filth and squalor. The threat of death by typhus, typhoid, or some other disease was always present. Inmates who became ill or were injured were reluctant to go to the camp hospital; they knew that there was little chance they would leave the hospital alive. The Nazis swept through the camp hospital on a regular basis, sending all patients, regardless of their health, to the gas chamber. Thus, many prisoners preferred to take their chances with disease or injury rather than risk being included in the next hospital selection for the gas chamber.

Selection

Primo Levi

> Jews in the concentration camps could not escape the threat of
> "selection," a regular occurrence in which prisoners were sent
> to the gas chambers. The Nazis used selections to weed out
> those inmates who were sick and no longer able to work or
> simply to make room for a new transport of prisoners, in which
> case, an entire barracks—sick and healthy alike—might be se-
> lected. Primo Levi, an Italian Jew, describes the panic that sets
> in among the sick and starving prisoners when rumors of a se-
> lection reach them. He writes of how inmates hasten to reas-
> sure each other about their appearance, lying brazenly about
> how they still look strong and healthy, even if they are actually
> a *musulmann* (camp slang for someone who is a walking skele-
> ton and likely to die soon). Levi explains how it is impossible
> for a prisoner to hide the fact that he is a *musulmann* as all in-
> mates involved in a selection must parade naked past SS offi-
> cers. In a split-second, the SS make the decision about who
> will live a while longer and who will not.

L ast spring [1943] the Germans had constructed huge
tents in an open space in the Lager [camp]. For the
whole of the good season each of them had catered for over
a thousand men: now the tents had been taken down, and an
excess two thousand guests crowded our huts. We old prisoners knew that the Germans did not like these irregularities and that something would soon happen to reduce our
number.

'Selekcja'

One feels the selections arriving. *'Selekcja':* the hybrid Latin and Polish word is heard once, twice, many times, interpolated in foreign conversations; at first we cannot distinguish it, then it forces itself on our attention, and in the end it persecutes us.

This morning the Poles had said *'Selekcja'.* The Poles are the first to find out the news, and they generally try not to let it spread around, because to know something which the others still do not know can always be useful. By the time that everyone realizes that a selection is imminent, the few possibilities of evading it (corrupting some doctor or some prominent with bread or tobacco; leaving the hut for Ka-Be [the infirmary] or vice-versa at the right moment so as to cross with the commission) are already their monopoly.

In the days which follow, the atmosphere of the Lager and the yard is filled with *'Selekcja':* nobody knows anything definite, but all speak about it, even the Polish, Italian, French civilian workers whom we secretly see in the yard. Yet the result is hardly a wave of despondency: our collective morale is too inarticulate and flat to be unstable. The fight against hunger, cold and work leaves little margin for thought, even for this thought. Everybody reacts in his own way, but hardly anyone with those attitudes which would seem the most plausible as the most realistic, that is with resignation or despair.

All those able to find a way out, try to take it; but they are the minority because it is very difficult to escape from a selection. The Germans apply themselves to these things with great skill and diligence.

'You Are All Right'

Whoever is unable to prepare for it materially, seeks defence elsewhere. In the latrines, in the washroom, we show each other our chests, our buttocks, our thighs, and our comrades reassure us: 'You are all right, it will certainly not be your turn this time, . . . *du bist kein Muselmann* [You are not a "muselmann," a skeletal, corpselike figure] . . . more probably mine . . .' and they undo their braces in turn and pull up their shirts.

Nobody refuses this charity to another: nobody is so sure of his own lot to be able to condemn others. I brazenly lied to old Wertheimer; I told him that if they questioned him, he should reply that he was forty-five, and he should not forget to have a shave the evening before, even if it cost him a quarter-ration of bread; apart from that he need have no fears, and in any case it was by no means certain that it was a selection for the gas chamber; had he not heard the *Blockältester* say that those chosen would go to Jaworszno to a convalescent camp?

It is absurd of Wertheimer to hope: he looks sixty, he has enormous varicose veins, he hardly even notices the hunger any more. But he lies down on his bed, serene and quiet, and replies to someone who asks him with my own words; they are the command-words in the camp these days: I myself repeated them just as—apart from details—Chajim told them to me, Chajim, who has been in Lager for three years, and being strong and robust is wonderfully sure of himself; and I believed them.

On this slender basis I also lived through the great selection of October 1944 with inconceivable tranquility. I was tranquil because I managed to lie to myself sufficiently. The fact that I was not selected depended above all on chance and does not prove that my faith was well-founded.

Monsieur Pinkert is also, a priori, condemned: it is enough to look at his eyes. He calls me over with a sign, and with a confidential air tells me that he has been informed— he cannot tell me the source of information—that this time there is really something new: the Holy See, by means of the International Red Cross . . . in short, he personally guarantees both for himself and for me, in the most absolute manner, that every danger is ruled out; as a civilian he was, as is well known, attaché to the Belgian embassy at Warsaw.

Thus in various ways, even those days of vigil, which in the telling seem as if they ought to have passed every limit of human torment, went by not very differently from other days.

The discipline in both the Lager and Buna [a nearby rubber factory where inmates provide slave labor] is in no way relaxed: the work, cold and hunger are sufficient to fill up every thinking moment.

The Day Arrives

Today is working Sunday, *Arbeitssonntag*: we work until 1 P.M., then we return to camp for the shower, shave and general control for skin diseases and lice. And in the yards, everyone knew mysteriously that the selection would be today.

The news arrived, as always, surrounded by a halo of contradictory or suspect details: the selection in the infirmary took place this morning; the percentage was seven per cent of the whole camp, thirty, fifty per cent of the patients. At Birkenau, the crematorium chimney has been smoking for ten days. Room has to be made for an enormous convoy arriving from the Poznan ghetto. The young tell the young that all the old ones will be chosen. The healthy tell the healthy that only the ill will be chosen. Specialists will be excluded. German Jews will be excluded. Low Numbers will be excluded. You will be chosen. I will be excluded.

At 1 P.M. exactly the yard empties in orderly fashion, and for two hours the grey unending army files past the two control stations where, as on every day, we are counted and recounted, and past the military band which for two hours without interruption plays, as on every day, those marches to which we must synchronize our steps at our entrance and our exit.

It seems like every day, the kitchen chimney smokes as usual, the distribution of the soup is already beginning. But then the bell is heard, and at that moment we realize that we have arrived.

Because this bell always sounds at dawn, when it means the reveille; but if it sounds during the day, it means *'Blocksperre'*, enclosure in huts, and this happens when there is a selection to prevent anyone avoiding it, or when those selected leave for the gas, to prevent anyone seeing them leave.

Waiting

Our *Blockältester* knows his business. He has made sure that we have all entered, he has the door locked, he has given everyone his card with his number, name, profession, age and nationality and he has ordered everyone to undress completely, except for shoes. We wait like this, naked, with the card in our hands, for the commission to reach our hut. We are hut 48, but one can never tell if they are going to begin at hut 1 or hut 60. At any rate, we can rest quietly at least for an hour, and there is no reason why we should not get under the blankets on the bunk and keep warm.

Many are already drowsing when a barrage of orders, oaths and blows proclaims the imminent arrival of the commission. The *Blockältester* and his helpers, starting at the end of the dormitory, drive the crowd of frightened, naked people in front of them and cram them in the *Tagesraum* which is the Quartermaster's office. The *Tagesraum* is a room seven yards by four: when the drive is over, a warm and compact human mass is jammed into the *Tagesraum*, perfectly filling all the corners, exercising such a pressure on the wooden walls as to make them creak.

Now we are all in the *Tagesraum*, and besides there being no time, there is not even any room in which to be afraid. The feeling of the warm flesh pressing all around is unusual and not unpleasant. One has to take care to hold up one's nose so as to breathe, and not to crumple or lose the card in one's hand.

A Life or Death Sentence

The *Blockältester* has closed the connecting-door and has opened the other two which lead from the dormitory and the

Tagesraum outside. Here, in front of the two doors, stands the arbiter of our fate, an SS subaltern. On his right is the *Blockältester,* on his left, the quartermaster of the hut. Each one of us, as he comes naked out of the *Tagesraum* into the cold October air, has to run the few steps between the two doors, give the card to the SS man and enter the dormitory door. The SS man, in the fraction of a second between two successive crossings, with a glance at one's back and front, judges everyone's fate, and in turn gives the card to the man on his right or his left, and this is the life or death of each of us. In three or four minutes a hut of two hundred men is 'done', as is the whole camp of twelve thousand men in the course of the afternoon.

Jammed in the charnel-house of the *Tagesraum,* I gradually felt the human pressure around me slacken, and in a short time it was my turn. Like everyone, I passed by with a brisk and elastic step, trying to hold my head high, my chest forward and my muscles contracted and conspicuous. With the corner of my eye I tried to look behind my shoulders, and my card seemed to end on the right.

As we gradually come back into the dormitory we are allowed to dress ourselves. Nobody yet knows with certainty his own fate, it has first of all to be established whether the condemned cards were those on the right or the left. By now there is no longer any point in sparing each other's feelings with superstitious scruples. Everybody crowds around the oldest, the most wasted-away, and most 'muselmann'; if their cards went to the left, the left is certainly the side of the condemned.

Irregularities and Mistakes

Even before the selection is over, everybody knows that the left was effectively the *'schlechte Seite'*, the bad side. There have naturally been some irregularities: René, for example, so young and robust, ended on the left; perhaps it was because he has glasses, perhaps because he walks a little stooped like a myope, but more probably because of a simple mistake: René passed the commission immediately in front of me and there could have been a mistake with our cards. I think about it, discuss it with Alberto, and we agree that the hypothesis is probable; I do not know what I will think tomorrow and later; today I feel no distinct emotion.

It must equally have been a mistake about Sattler, a huge Transylvanian peasant who was still at home only twenty days ago; Sattler does not understand German, he has understood nothing of what has taken place, and stands in a corner mending his shirt. Must I go and tell him that his shirt will be of no more use?

There is nothing surprising about these mistakes: the examination is too quick and summary, and in any case, the important thing for the Lager is not that the most useless prisoners be eliminated, but that free posts be quickly created, according to a certain percentage previously fixed.

Double Rations for the Chosen

The selection is now over in our hut, but it continues in the others, so that we are still locked in. But as the soup-pots have arrived in the meantime, the *Blockältester* decides to proceed with the distribution at once. A double ration will be given to those selected. I have never discovered if this was a ridiculously charitable initiative of the *Blockältester,* or an explicit disposition of the SS, but in fact, in the interval of two or three days (sometimes even much longer) between the selection and the departure, the victims at Monowitz-Auschwitz enjoyed this privilege.

Ziegler holds out his bowl, collects his normal ration and then waits there expectantly. 'What do you want?' asks the *Blockältester*: according to him, Ziegler is entitled to no supplement, and he drives him away, but Ziegler returns and humbly persists. He was on the left, everybody saw it, let the *Blockältester* check the cards; he has the right to a double ration. When he is given it, he goes quietly to his bunk to eat.

Now everyone is busy scraping the bottom of his bowl with his spoon so as not to waste the last drops of the soup; a confused, metallic clatter, signifying the end of the day. Silence slowly prevails and then, from my bunk on the top row, I see and hear old Kuhn praying aloud, with his beret on his head, swaying backwards and forwards violently. Kuhn is thanking God because he has not been chosen.

Kuhn is out of his senses. Does he not see Beppo the Greek in the bunk next to him, Beppo who is twenty years old and is going to the gas chamber the day after tomorrow and knows it and lies there looking fixedly at the light without saying anything and without even thinking any more? Can Kuhn fail to realize that next time it will be his turn? Does Kuhn not understand that what has happened today is an abomination, which no propitiatory prayer, no pardon, no expiation by the guilty, which nothing at all in the power of man can ever clean again?

If I was God, I would spit at Kuhn's prayer.

Murdering Babies

Sara Nomberg-Przytyk

When prisoners arrived at the extermination camps, the Nazis immediately sent women who were obviously pregnant to the gas chambers. However, a few pregnant women managed to escape detection and gave birth in the camps. Sara Nomberg-Przytyk worked as a nurse in the infirmary at Auschwitz, and in the following essay she describes what happened to the women who gave birth and their newborns.

Joseph Mengele, the chief Nazi physician at Auschwitz, believed he was being compassionate when he sent all mothers and their children to the gas chambers; he claimed the camps were no place for babies and children and therefore it was only humanitarian to allow a mother to be with her child when it was killed. Nomberg-Przytyk writes that the doctors and nurses who worked in the camp infirmaries were well aware of Mengele's policy; in order to save the mother's life, they insisted that the woman give birth in secret and then they killed the baby as soon as it was born. However, she reports that one Jewish woman refused to believe that Mengele would kill her baby and insisted on giving birth openly in the camp hospital and proudly showed off her baby to Mengele when he came by during a selection.

One warm April day Esther came to the infirmary. She approached me and said very quietly, "I have a very important matter to discuss with you. Can we discuss it privately?"

I knew Esther from the Bialystok Ghetto. On 16 August 1943, the Bialystok Ghetto had been liquidated. For three

Excerpted from *Auschwitz: True Tales from a Grotesque Land*, by Sara Nomberg-Przytyk, edited by Eli Pfefferkorn and David H. Hirsch. Translated by Roslyn Hirsch. Copyright © 1985 by the University of North Carolina Press. Used by permission of the publisher.

months Esther, her husband, her mother, and a five-year-old niece who perished in Slonim [in Poland], hid with me in a bunker built in my apartment. At the time she was a young woman. I doubt that she was even twenty years old. She had a pretty face but it was not an interesting one. I remember that in the bunker we had a lot of trouble with her, because she had no talents and could not be counted on to help out. When the German gendarmes discovered our bunker they shot her husband on the spot. As soon as the three females arrived at Auschwitz, the Germans took away the little girl whom she had cared for affectionately, and a few months later her mother was taken at a selection. Esther was alone in Auschwitz.

She stood before me, now, peculiarly thick, red in the face and a little embarrassed. Maybe she was pregnant.

Pregnant

"As you can see for yourself," she blurted out, "I am going to give birth any day now. All this time I've been going to work, but now I want to stay in the hospital. I want to give birth to this baby. It's my first baby. It moves. It kicks me. It will probably be a son. My husband is not here anymore. That's his son. Please help me," she ended her pleading.

I turned to stone. Didn't she know what [SS Dr. Joseph] Mengele did to women who had babies in the camp? I looked into her happy eyes and at her enraptured features. For the first minute I really did not know what to tell her. Could I extinguish the happiness that emanated from her whole body? Or maybe I should just say nothing. Maybe I should let her live through her great love for her first baby and let the worst come later.

Why Jewish Children Must Be Killed

Orli had told me once how Mengele explained to her why he killed Jewish women together with their children. "When a Jewish child is born, or when a woman comes to the camp with a child already," he had explained, "I don't know what to do with the child. I can't set the child free because there are no longer any Jews who live in freedom. I can't let the child stay in the camp because there are no facilities in the camp that would enable the child to develop normally. It would not be humanitarian to send a child to the ovens without permitting the mother to be there to witness the child's death. That is why I send the mother and the child to the gas ovens together."

Imagine that cynical criminal justifying his hideous crimes in the name of humanitarianism, making a mockery of the tenderest of all feelings, a mother's love for her children.

I had seen the conditions under which Jewish women gave birth in the camp. A doctor from the infirmary took me to one of the births. "Come with me," she said. "Join me in witnessing the crimes of Auschwitz and the depths of human suffering."

On our way to the block in field "B" Mancy told me that the women who were due to deliver were not taken to the infirmary. The delivery took place in the block where the woman lived. "You see," she said, "the birth has to take place in secrecy. Nobody is supposed to know about it. In the hospital block it is impossible to conceal the birth of a child from the Germans. Our procedure now is to kill the baby after birth in such a way that the mother doesn't know about it."

"What? You kill it?" I stopped in the middle of the path.

"It's very simple," Mancy continued. "We give the baby an injection. After that, the baby dies. The mother is told that the baby was born dead. After dark, the baby is thrown on a pile of corpses, and in that manner we save the mother. I want so much for the babies to be born dead, but out of spite they are born healthy. I simply don't know why the children are healthy. The pregnant women do heavy work till the last day; there is no food; and in spite of it all, the children are healthy. My worry now is that I don't have any injections left."

A Secret Birth

It was already dark when we arrived at the block. The women took us to the woman in labor. Mancy told her to lie on the ground under the board bed. She herself hid there too. "Remember," she said to her quietly, "you are forbidden to utter a sound. Everything has to take place in complete silence. Nobody should know that you are giving birth." She told me to bring her a bucket of cold water. She put it next to her.

"Sit next to me. You will be my helper," she said to me.

Two women stood near the bed. One of them was guarding the entrance to the block.

The birth started. The woman bit her lips in pain until she drew blood. But she did not utter even one sound. She held my hands so tightly that afterwards I had black and blue marks. Finally, the baby was born. Mancy put her hand over his mouth so he would not cry, and then she put his head in the bucket of cold water. She was drowning him like a blind kitten. I felt faint. I had to get out from under the bed.

"The baby was born dead," Mancy said. Later, she wrapped the dead baby in an old shirt, and the woman who was guarding the entrance took the baby and left to put it on a pile of corpses. The mother was saved.

Telling the Truth

Right then Esther, who knew nothing, was standing in front of me, wanting to go to the hospital to give birth to a baby like thousands of other women in the world. She was listening to the movements of her baby and was happy. She did not know that if a German doctor found out she would die with her baby. I decided to tell her everything.

"You see, Esther," I started, "you can't give birth to a living baby. It must die before anybody finds out about it. Otherwise, you will die with it."

"What? A dead baby? I want to have a live baby. I am sure that when Mengele sees it he will let me raise it in the camp. It is going to be a beauty because my husband was very handsome. You knew him. I want to have it in the infirmary."

Mancy and Marusia talked to her, but without success. The same day she went to the infirmary, and that night she gave birth to a beautiful baby boy.

She lay there in bed with the baby, very happy. The attendants tried to convince her not to feed the baby so that it would die of hunger. Esther would not hear of it. She gave the baby her breast and talked with wonder about how beautifully it suckled. The supervisor of the infirmary had a duty to report all births, but somehow she delayed. She had pity on Esther.

On the third day of Esther's stay in the hospital block, the first day of the Passover holiday, a big selection took place. I was on the block when Mengele and an SS man came in. They both stood on the stove. The gate was bolted, and every sick woman was paraded naked in front of them. In his tightly closed fist Mengele held a pencil whose point stuck out a little way from his palm. The SS man read, and at the same time, wrote down the numbers, while Mengele pushed the pencil into his fist with a slow movement of his thumb. This meant death. The red-headed SS man put down a cross next to the designated number. Finally, Esther's turn came. She went naked, and in her arms she held the baby. She held it up high as though she wanted to show them what a beautiful and healthy son she had. Mengele slowly pushed the pencil into his clenched fist.

The Twins Experiments

Miklos Nyiszli

> Joseph Mengele is infamous as the chief Nazi doctor at the
> Auschwitz concentration camps. Not only did he make the
> initial selections as new prisoners arrived at Auschwitz, he
> also was responsible for cruel and sadistic "experiments" per-
> formed on the inmates. One of the experiments he oversaw
> was an attempt to change a person's eye color by injecting
> dye into the iris. Mengele was also fascinated with dwarfs
> and twins, and performed many painful and traumatic experi-
> ments on them.
>
> Mengele used doctors who were prisoners in Auschwitz to
> help him with his experiments. Miklos Nyiszli, a Jewish Greek
> doctor who was transported to Auschwitz in 1944, volunteered
> to be Mengele's personal research pathologist. Nyiszli's duties
> included performing autopsies on camp prisoners who died
> during or were killed after Mengele's experiments. In the fol-
> lowing essay, Nyiszli discusses some of the autopsies he per-
> formed on twins who were subjected to Mengele's experiments.

When the convoys arrived, soldiers scouted the ranks
lined up before the box cars, hunting for twins and
dwarfs. Mothers, hoping for special treatment for their twin
children, readily gave them up to the scouts. Adult twins,
knowing that they were of interest from a scientific point of
view, voluntarily presented themselves, in the hope of better treatment. The same for dwarfs.

Excerpted from *Auschwitz: A Doctor's Eyewitness Account*, by Miklos Nyiszli (New
York: Seaver Books, 1960). Copyright © 1960 by N. Margareta Nyiszli. Translation
copyright © 1993 by Richard Seaver. Reprinted by permission of Arcade Publishing,
New York, N.Y.

They were separated from the rest and herded to the right. They were allowed to keep their civilian clothes; guards accompanied them to specially designed barracks, where they were treated with a certain regard. Their food was good, their bunks were comfortable, and possibilities for hygiene were provided.

The Experiments

They were housed in Barracks 14 of Camp F. From there they were taken by their guards to the experimentation barracks of the Gypsy Camp, and exposed to every medical examination that can be performed on human beings: blood tests, lumbar punctures, exchanges of blood between twin brothers, as well as numerous other examinations, all fatiguing and depressing. Dina, the painter from Prague, made the comparative studies of the structure of the twins' skulls, ears, noses, mouths, hands and feet. Each drawing was classified in a file set up for that express purpose, complete with all individual characteristics; into this file would also go the final results of this research. The procedure was the same for the dwarfs.

The experiments, in medical language called *in vivo,* i.e., experiments performed on live human beings, were far from exhausting the research possibilities in the study of twins. Full of lacunae, they offered no better than partial results. The *in vivo* experiments were succeeded by the most important phase of twin-study: the comparative examination from the viewpoints of anatomy and pathology. Here it was a question of comparing the twins' healthy organs with those functioning abnormally, or of comparing their illnesses. For that study, as for all studies of a pathological nature, corpses were needed. Since it was necessary to perform a dissection for the simultaneous evaluation of anomalies, the twins had to die at the same time. So it was that they met their death in the B section of one of Auschwitz's KZ barracks, at the hand of Dr. Mengele.

This phenomenon was unique in world medical science history. Twin brothers died together, and it was possible to perform autopsies on both. Where, under normal circumstances, can one find twin brothers who die at the same place and at the same time? For twins, like everyone else, are separated by life's varying circumstances. They live far from each other and almost never die simultaneously. One may die at the age of ten, the other at fifty. Under such conditions comparative dissection is impossible. In the Auschwitz camp, however, there were several hundred sets of twins, and therefore as many possibilities of dissection. That was why, on the arrival platform, Dr. Mengele separated twins and dwarfs from the other prisoners. That was why both special groups were directed to the right-hand column, and thence to the barracks of the spared. That was why they had good food and hygienic living conditions, so that they didn't contaminate each other and die one before the other. They had to die together, and in good health.

Twin Dissections

The Sonderkommando chief came hunting for me and announced that an SS soldier was waiting for me at the door of the crematorium with a crew of corpse-transporting kommandos. I went in search of them, for they were forbidden to enter the courtyard. I took the documents concerning the corpses from the hands of the SS. They contained files on two little twin brothers. The kommando crew, made up entirely of women, set the covered coffin down in front of me. I lifted the lid. Inside lay a set of two-year-old twins. I ordered two of my men to take the corpses and place them on the dissecting table.

I opened the file and glanced through it. Very detailed clinical examinations, accompanied by X-rays, descriptions, and artists' drawings, indicated from the scientific viewpoint the different aspects of these two little beings' "twinhood." Only the pathological report was missing. It was my job to supply it. The twins had died at the same time and were now lying beside each other on the big dissecting table. It was they who had to—or whose tiny bodies had to—resolve the secret of the reproduction of the race. To advance one step in the search to unlock the secret of multiplying the race of superior beings destined to rule was a "noble goal." If only it were possible, in the future, to have each German mother bear as many twins as possible! The project, conceived by the demented theorists of the Third Reich, was utterly mad. And it was to Dr. Mengele, chief physician of the Auschwitz KZ, the notorious "criminal doctor," that these experiments had been entrusted.

Among malefactors and criminals, the most dangerous type is the "criminal doctor," especially when he is armed with powers such as those granted to Dr. Mengele. He sent millions of people to death merely because, according to a racial theory, they were inferior beings and therefore detrimental to mankind. This same criminal doctor spent long hours beside me, either at his microscopes, his disinfecting ovens and his test tubes or, standing with equal patience near the dissecting table, his smock befouled with blood, his bloody hands examining and experimenting like one possessed. The immediate objective was the increased reproduction of the German race. The final objective was the production of pure Germans in numbers sufficient to replace the Czechs, Hungarians, Poles, all of whom were condemned to be destroyed, but who for the moment were living on those territories declared vital to the Third Reich.

I finished the dissection of the little twins and wrote out a regulation report of the dissection. I did my job well and my chief appeared to be satisfied with me. But he had some trouble reading my handwriting, for all my letters were capitals, a habit I had picked up in America. And so I told him that if he wanted clear clean copy, he would have to supply me with a typewriter, since I was accustomed to work with one in my own practice.

"What make typewriter are you used to?" he asked.

"Olympia Elite," I said.

"Very well, I'll send you one. You'll have it tomorrow. I want clean copy, because these reports will be forwarded to the Institute of Biological, Racial and Evolutionary Research at Berlin-Dahlem."

Thus I learned that the experiments performed here were checked by the highest medical authorities at one of the most famous scientific institutes in the world.

Four More Pairs of Twins

The following day an SS soldier brought me an "Olympia" typewriter. Still more corpses of twins were sent to me. They delivered me four pairs from the Gypsy Camp; all four were under ten years old.

I began the dissection of one set of twins and recorded each phase of my work. I removed the brain pan. Together with the cerebellum I extracted the brain and examined them. Then fol-

A Victim of One of Mengele's Experiments

Many victims of Joseph Mengele's experiments never lived to tell the world about what they experienced; they were frequently killed afterward so that their bodies could be autopsied and examined to see what effect, if any, the experiment had on them. Irene Zisblatt, an experiment victim, escaped execution. Here, she briefly recounts a few of the experiments she was forced to endure while at Auschwitz.

I went through four experiments. The first time Mengele examined our naked bodies to make sure we didn't have any blemishes before five of us were taken to Auschwitz, next to Birkenau, and had drops put in our eyes. We were then put in a dungeon, like a tiny cubicle, where we were standing in water up to our ankles; with the door closed it was pitch dark. I don't know how long we were in there—three days, five days or one day, or perhaps one hour—it seemed like forever. They never opened the door and they never gave us anything to eat

lowed the opening of the thorax and the removal of the sternum. Next I separated the tongue by means of an incision made beneath the chin. With the tongue came the esophagus, with the respiratory tracts came both lungs. I washed the organs in order to examine them more thoroughly. The tiniest spot or the slightest difference in color could furnish valuable information. I made a transverse incision across the pericardium and removed the fluid. Next I took out the heart and washed it. I turned it over and over in my hand to examine it.

A Monstrous Secret

In the exterior coat of the left ventricle was a small pale red spot caused by a hypodermic injection, which scarcely differed from the color of the tissue around it. There could be no mistake. The injection had been given with a very small needle. Without a doubt a hypodermic needle. For what

---

or drink, so we drank the water we stood in. We went to the bathroom in the water we stood in. Then they took us out and examined our eyes and took us back to the barracks; some couldn't see for several days after. We found out later that they were trying to change the colour of our eyes. . . . A few days later I was selected again for another experiment. This time they strapped us to a rusty, dirty table, injected something into the numbers tattooed on our arms and began to cut, without anaesthetic. Half of the time we didn't know what they were doing because we were unconscious from the pain. There was a nurse there and she was filling out papers and keeping records. Afterwards the nurse—who was Jewish— was told to give us a lethal injection, but she saved our lives by putting us in the tuberculosis room—she knew that the doctors and Gestapo would not go in there because it was contagious—and then taking us to a different barrack so we wouldn't be recognised.

Irene Zisblatt, in *The Last Days,* presented by Steven Spielberg and Survivors of the Shoah Visual History Foundation. New York: St. Martin's Press, 1999.

purpose had he received the injection? Injections into the heart can be administered in extremely serious cases, when the heart begins to fail. I would soon know. I opened the heart, starting with the ventricle. Normally the blood contained in the left ventricle is taken out and weighed. This method could not be employed in the present case, because the blood was coagulated into a compact mass. I extracted the coagulum with the forceps and brought it to my nose. I was struck by the characteristic odor of chloroform. The victim had received an injection of chloroform in the heart, so that the blood of the ventricle, in coagulating, would deposit on the valves and cause instantaneous death by heart failure.

My discovery of the most monstrous secret of the Third Reich's medical science made my knees tremble. Not only did they kill with gas, but also with injections of chloroform into the heart. A cold sweat broke out on my forehead. Luckily I was alone. If others had been present it would have been difficult for me to conceal my excitement. I finished the dissection, noted the differences found, and recorded them. But the chloroform, the blood coagulated in the left ventricle, the puncture visible in the external coat of the heart, did not figure among my findings. It was a useful precaution on my part. Dr. Mengele's records on the subject of twins were in my hands. They contained the exact examinations, X-rays, the artist's sketches already mentioned, but neither the circumstances nor causes of death. Nor did I fill out that column of the dissection report. It was not a good idea to exceed the authorized bounds of knowledge or to relate all one had witnessed. And here still less than anywhere else. I was not timorous by nature and my nerves were good. During my medical practice I had often brought to light the causes of death. I had seen the bodies of people assassinated for motives of revenge, jealousy, or material gain, as well as those of suicides and natural deaths. I was used to the study of well-hidden causes of death. On several occasions I had been shocked by my discoveries, but now a shudder of fear ran through me. If Dr. Mengele had any idea that I had discovered the secret of his injections he would send ten doctors, in the name of the political SS, to attest to my death.

Special Files

In accordance with orders received I returned the corpses to the prisoners whose duty it was to burn them. They performed their job without delay. I had to keep any organs of possible scientific interest, so that Dr. Mengele could examine them. Those which might interest the Anthropological Institute at Berlin-Dahlem were preserved in alcohol. These parts were specially packed to be sent through the mails. Stamped "War Material—Urgent," they were given top priority in transit. In the course of my work at the crematorium I dispatched an impressive number of such packages. I received, in reply, either precise scientific observations or instructions. In order to classify this correspondence I had to set up special files. The directors of the Berlin-Dahlem Institute always warmly thanked Dr. Mengele for this rare and precious material.

I finished dissecting the three other pairs of twins and duly recorded the anomalies found. In all three instances the cause of death was the same: an injection of chloroform into the heart.

Of the four sets of twins, three had ocular globes of different colors. One eye was brown, the other blue. This is a phenomenon found fairly frequently in non-twins. But in the present case I noticed that it had occurred in six out of the eight twins. An extremely interesting collection of anomalies. Medical science calls them heterochromes, which means, merely, different-colored. I cut out the eyes and put them in a solution of formaldehyde, noting their characteristics exactly in order not to mix them up. During my examination of the four sets of twins, I discovered still another curious phenomenon: while removing the skin from the neck I noticed, just above the upper extremity of the sternum, a tumor about the size of a small nut. Pressing on it with my forceps I found it to be filled with a thick pus.

This rare manifestation, well known to medical science, indicates the presence of hereditary syphilis and is called DuBois' tumor. Looking farther, I found that it existed in all eight twins. I cut out the tumor, leaving it surrounded by healthy tissue, and placed it in another jar of formaldehyde. In two sets of twins I also discovered evidence of active, cavernous tuberculosis. I recorded my findings on the dissection report, but left the heading "Cause of Death" blank.

Cause of Death

During the afternoon Dr. Mengele paid me a visit. I gave him a detailed account of my morning's work and handed him my report. He sat down and began to read each case carefully. He was greatly interested by the heterochromatic condition of the eyes, but even more so by the discovery of DuBois' tumor. He gave me instructions to have the organs mailed and told me to include my report in the package. He also instructed me to fill out the "Cause of Death" column hitherto left blank. The choice of causes was left to my own judgment and discretion; the only stipulation was that each cause be different. Almost apologetically he remarked that, as I could see for myself, these children were syphilitic and tubercular, and consequently would not have lived in any case. . . . He said no more about it. With that he had said enough. He had explained the reason for these children's death. I had refrained from making any comment. But I had learned that here tuberculosis and syphilis were not treated with medicines and drugs, but with chloroform injections.

I shuddered to think of all I had learned during my short stay here, and of all I should yet have to witness without protesting, until my own appointed hour arrived. The minute I entered this place I had the feeling I was already one of the living-dead. But now, in possession of all these fantastic secrets, I was certain I would never get out alive. Was it conceivable that Dr. Mengele, or the Berlin-Dahlem Institute, would ever allow me to leave this place alive?

A Relief When Father Dies

Elie Wiesel

Many families were split apart when they arrived at the concentration camps; those who were strong and in the prime of their life watched helplessly as parents, grandparents, young children, and frail or ill relatives were led off to be executed. Some prisoners were luckier; they were able to stay together with at least one family member or friend. Often the fact that a prisoner had someone else to look after gave them the strength, drive, and courage to stay alive. Sometimes, however, the energy required to try and keep two people alive was simply too much for a prisoner who was on the brink of death himself.

In the following essay, Elie Wiesel, a noted author, survivor of the Holocaust, and the 1986 Nobel Peace Prize laureate, relates the struggle of keeping his dying father alive after they were forced to march from Auschwitz to the Buchenwald concentration camp in 1945. While part of Wiesel wants his father to live, another part secretly hopes that he will die. Wiesel dreams of being able to eat his father's food ration and using all his energy to save himself. When his father finally does die, Wiesel was pained that he did not feel grief and that what he did feel was, in fact, relief.

At the gate of the camp, SS officers were waiting for us. They counted us. Then we were directed to the assembly place. Orders were given us through loudspeakers:

"Form fives!" "Form groups of a hundred!" "Five paces forward!"

Excerpted from *Night* by Elie Wiesel, translated by Stella Rodway. Copyright © 1960 by MacGibbon & Kee. Copyright renewed 1988 by The Collins Publishing Group. Reprinted by permission of Hill and Wang, a division of Farrar, Straus and Giroux, LLC.

I held onto my father's hand—the old, familiar fear: not to lose him.

Right next to us the high chimney of the crematory oven rose up. It no longer made any impression on us. It scarcely attracted our attention.

An established inmate of Buchenwald told us that we should have a shower and then we could go into the blocks. The idea of having a hot bath fascinated me. My father was silent. He was breathing heavily beside me.

"Father," I said. "Only another moment more. Soon we can lie down—in a bed. You can rest. . . ."

He did not answer. I was so exhausted myself that his silence left me indifferent. My only wish was to take a bath as quickly as possible and lie down in a bed.

But it was not easy to reach the showers. Hundreds of prisoners were crowding there. The guards were unable to keep any order. They struck out right and left with no apparent result. Others, without the strength to push or even to stand up, had sat down in the snow. My father wanted to do the same. He groaned.

"I can't go on. . . . This is the end. . . . I'm going to die here. . . ."

He dragged me toward a hillock of snow from which emerged human shapes and ragged pieces of blanket.

"Leave me," he said to me. "I can't go on. . . . Have mercy on me. . . . I'll wait here until we can get into the baths. . . . You can come and find me."

I could have wept with rage. Having lived through so much, suffered so much, could I leave my father to die now? Now, when we could have a good hot bath and lie down?

"Father!" I screamed. "Father! Get up from here! Immediately! You're killing yourself. . . ."

I seized him by the arm. He continued to groan.

"Don't shout, son. . . . Take pity on your old father. . . . Leave me to rest here. . . . Just for a bit, I'm so tired . . . at the end of my strength. . . ."

He had become like a child, weak, timid, vulnerable.

"Father," I said. "You can't stay here."

I showed him the corpses all around him; they too had wanted to rest here.

"I can see them, son. I can see them all right. Let them sleep. It's so long since they closed their eyes. . . . They are exhausted . . . exhausted. . . ."

His voice was tender.

I yelled against the wind:

"They'll never wake again! Never! Don't you understand?"

For a long time this argument went on. I felt that I was not arguing with him, but with death itself, with the death that he had already chosen.

The sirens began to wail. An alert. The lights went out throughout the camp. The guards drove us toward the blocks. In a flash, there was no one left on the assembly place. We were only too glad not to have had to stay outside longer in the icy wind. We let ourselves sink down onto the planks. The beds were in several tiers. The cauldrons of soup at the entrance attracted no one. To sleep, that was all that mattered.

It was daytime when I awoke. And then I remembered that I had a father. Since the alert, I had followed the crowd without troubling about him. I had known that he was at the end, on the brink of death, and yet I had abandoned him.

I went to look for him.

But at the same moment this thought came into my mind: "Don't let me find him! If only I could get rid of this dead weight, so that I could use all my strength to struggle for my own survival, and only worry about myself." Immediately I felt ashamed of myself, ashamed forever.

I walked for hours without finding him. Then I came to the block where they were giving out black "coffee." The men were lining up and fighting.

A plaintive, beseeching voice caught me in the spine:

"Eliezer ... my son ... bring me ... a drop of coffee. ..."

I ran to him.

"Father! I've been looking for you for so long. . . . Where were you? Did you sleep? . . . How do you feel?"

He was burning with fever. Like a wild beast, I cleared a way for myself to the coffee cauldron. And I managed to carry back a cupful. I had a sip. The rest was for him. I can't forget the light of thankfulness in his eyes while he gulped it down—an animal gratitude. With those few gulps of hot water, I probably brought him more satisfaction than I had done during my whole childhood.

He was lying on a plank, livid, his lips pale and dried up, shaken by tremors. I could not stay by him for long. Orders had been given to clear the place for cleaning. Only the sick could stay.

We stayed outside for five hours. Soup was given out. As soon as we were allowed to go back to the blocks, I ran to my father.

"Have you had anything to eat?"

"No."

"Why not?"

"They didn't give us anything . . . they said that if we were ill we should die soon anyway and it would be a pity to waste the food. I can't go on any more. . . ."

I gave him what was left of my soup. But it was with a heavy heart. I felt that I was giving it up to him against my will. No better than Rabbi Eliahou's son had I withstood the test.

He grew weaker day by day, his gaze veiled, his face the color of dead leaves. On the third day after our arrival at Buchenwald, everyone had to go to the showers. Even the sick, who had to go through last.

On the way back from the baths, we had to wait outside for a long time. They had not yet finished cleaning the blocks.

Seeing my father in the distance, I ran to meet him. He went by me like a ghost, passed me without stopping, without looking at me. I called to him. He did not come back. I ran after him:

"Father, where are you running to?"

He looked at me for a moment, and his gaze was distant, visionary; it was the face of someone else. A moment only and on he ran again.

Struck down with dysentery, my father lay in his bunk, five other invalids with him. I sat by his side, watching him, not daring to believe that he could escape death again. Nevertheless, I did all I could to give him hope.

Suddenly, he raised himself on his bunk and put his feverish lips to my ear:

"Eliezer . . . I must tell you where to find the gold and the money I buried . . . in the cellar. . . . You know. . . ."

He began to talk faster and faster, as though he were afraid he would not have time to tell me. I tried to explain to him that this was not the end, that we would go back to the house together, but he would not listen to me. He could no longer listen to me. He was exhausted. A trickle of saliva, mingled with blood, was running from between his lips. He had closed his eyes. His breath was coming in gasps.

For a ration of bread, I managed to change beds with a prisoner in my father's bunk. In the afternoon the doctor came. I went and told him that my father was very ill.

"Bring him here!"

I explained that he could not stand up. But the doctor refused to listen to anything. Somehow, I brought my father to him. He stared at him, then questioned him in a clipped voice:

"What do you want?"

"My father's ill," I answered for him. "Dysentery . . ."

"Dysentery? That's not my business. I'm a surgeon. Go on! Make room for the others."

Protests did no good.

"I can't go on, son. . . . Take me back to my bunk. . . ."

I took him back and helped him to lie down. He was shivering.

"Try and sleep a bit, father. Try to go to sleep. . . ."

His breathing was labored, thick. He kept his eyes shut. Yet I was convinced that he could see everything, that now he could see the truth in all things.

Another doctor came to the block. But my father would not get up. He knew that it was useless.

Besides, this doctor had only come to finish off the sick. I could hear him shouting at them that they were lazy and just wanted to stay in bed. I felt like leaping at his throat, strangling him. But I no longer had the courage or the strength. I was riveted to my father's deathbed. My hands hurt, I was clenching them so hard. Oh, to strangle the doctor and the others! To burn the whole world! My father's murderers! But the cry stayed in my throat.

When I came back from the bread distribution, I found my father weeping like a child:

"Son, they keep hitting me!"

"Who?"

I thought he was delirious.

"Him, the Frenchman . . . and the Pole . . . they were hitting me."

Another wound to the heart, another hate, another reason for living lost.

"Eliezer . . . Eliezer . . . tell them not to hit me. . . . I haven't done anything. . . . Why do they keep hitting me?"

I began to abuse his neighbors. They laughed at me. I promised them bread, soup. They laughed. Then they got angry; they could not stand my father any longer, they said, because he was now unable to drag himself outside to relieve himself.

The following day he complained that they had taken his ration of bread.

"While you were asleep?"

"No. I wasn't asleep. They jumped on top of me. They snatched my bread . . . and they hit me . . . again. . . . I can't stand any more, son . . . a drop of water. . . ."

I knew that he must not drink. But he pleaded with me for

so long that I gave in. Water was the worst poison he could have, but what else could I do for him? With water, without water, it would all be over soon anyway. . . .

"You, at least, have some mercy on me. . . ."

Have mercy on him! I, his only son!

A week went by like this.

"This is your father, isn't it?" asked the head of the block.

"Yes."

"He's very ill."

"The doctor won't do anything for him."

"The doctor *can't* do anything for him, now. And neither can you."

He put his great hairy hand on my shoulder and added:

"Listen to me, boy. Don't forget that you're in a concentration camp. Here, every man has to fight for himself and not think of anyone else. Even of his father. Here, there are no fathers, no brothers, no friends. Everyone lives and dies for himself alone. I'll give you a sound piece of advice— don't give your ration of bread and soup to your old father. There's nothing you can do for him. And you're killing yourself. Instead, you ought to be having his ration."

I listened to him without interrupting. He was right, I thought in the most secret region of my heart, but I dared not admit it. It's too late to save your old father, I said to myself. You ought to be having two rations of bread, two rations of soup. . . .

Only a fraction of a second, but I felt guilty. I ran to find a little soup to give my father. But he did not want it. All he wanted was water.

"Don't drink water . . . have some soup. . . ."

"I'm burning . . . why are you being so unkind to me, my son? Some water. . . ."

I brought him some water. Then I left the block for roll call. But I turned around and came back again. I lay down on the top bunk. Invalids were allowed to stay in the block. So I would be an invalid myself. I would not leave my father.

There was silence all round now, broken only by groans. In front of the block, the SS were giving orders. An officer passed by the beds. My father begged me:

"My son, some water. I'm burning. . . . My stomach. . . ."

"Quiet, over there!" yelled the officer.

"Eliezer," went on my father, "some water. . . ."

The officer came up to him and shouted at him to be quiet. But my father did not hear him. He went on calling me. The officer dealt him a violent blow on the head with his truncheon.

I did not move. I was afraid. My body was afraid of also receiving a blow.

Then my father made a rattling noise and it was my name: "Eliezer."

I could see that he was still breathing—spasmodically.

I did not move.

When I got down after roll call, I could see his lips trembling as he murmured something. Bending over him, I stayed gazing at him for over an hour, engraving into myself the picture of his blood-stained face, his shattered skull.

Then I had to go to bed. I climbed into my bunk, above my father, who was still alive. It was January 28, 1945.

I awoke on January 29 at dawn. In my father's place lay another invalid. They must have taken him away before dawn and carried him to the crematory. He may still have been breathing.

There were no prayers at his grave. No candles were lit to his memory. His last word was my name. A summons, to which I did not respond.

I did not weep, and it pained me that I could not weep. But I had no more tears. And, in the depths of my being, in the recesses of my weakened conscience, could I have searched it, I might perhaps have found something like—free at last!

Chapter 5

The Germans

Chapter Preface

The prisoners in the concentration camps were guarded by several different groups. At the top of the hierarchy were the *Schutzstaffel,* known as the SS, an elite guard originally formed to protect Adolf Hitler. Most of the other guards were German or Ukrainian soldiers. Below them were the prisoners who were put in charge of their fellow inmates: *lagerälteste,* the camp elder, the highest-ranking prisoner in camp; *blockälteste,* the chief inmate responsible for a barracks or a block; and *kapo,* Italian for the head of work detail. Although the inmate leaders tended to be violent criminals, most of the other guards had led ordinary lives before the war, as farmers, salesmen, nurses, or factory workers, for example. Some volunteered for their service, while others were drafted. Yet when these ordinary people—Germans, Ukrainians, and inmates—were put in charge of thousands of Jews, political prisoners, Gypsies, Poles, and other "undesirables," many became extraordinarily sadistic and brutal toward anyone in their power, especially the Jews.

After years of anti-Semitic propaganda, many of the concentration camp guards felt they were performing a service by ridding the world of Jews and other "subhuman" beings who were biologically inferior to the Aryan race. Others took pride in their work, noting how quickly and accurately they killed their prisoners. Some Germans believed they were just following orders, doing their duty for their country in the best way they could.

However, a few—guards and civilians—were kind to the prisoners. Occasionally, guards would turn a blind eye to prisoners' dealings or even help them in their efforts to gain food and clothing. Many inmates' lives were saved by civilians who took pity on them and smuggled in food and valuables despite the great risk to themselves.

Auschwitz: The Greatest Extermination Center

Rudolf Höss

> Rudolf Höss was the commandant of the extermination camps
> at Auschwitz from May 1940 to December 1943, when he left
> to become chief of the Inspectorate of Concentration Camps,
> an agency which oversaw the running of the concentration
> camps. Höss, as a witness at the Nuremberg Trials, testified
> that 2.5 million Jews died in the gas chambers at Auschwitz,
> and approximately another 500,000 died from starvation and
> disease. The number of Jews who died in the gas chambers at
> Auschwitz has since been reduced to 1.5 million. The follow-
> ing essay is an excerpt from his autobiography which he wrote
> while awaiting trial in Poland in 1946 for his war crimes.
>
> Höss writes that he was just following orders from Hein-
> rich Himmler, head of the Gestapo and second in command
> in Germany, and Adolf Hitler, Germany's leader, when he
> gassed the millions of Jews in the camps. He claims that as
> an officer of the SS, he could not question his orders, nor
> should he, as he was not privy to all the reasons that made the
> order necessary. In fact, he notes, the order to exterminate the
> Jews seemed perfectly reasonable to him.
>
> Poland convicted Höss of war crimes and hanged him at
> Auschwitz on April 16, 1947.

Excerpted from *Commandant of Auschwitz: The Autobiography of Rudolf Hoess*, with an
introduction by Lord Russell of Liverpool. Translated from the German by Constantine
FitzGibbon (Cleveland: World Publishing, 1959). English translation © 1959 by Weidenfeld & Nicolson Ltd. Reprinted by permission of Weidenfeld & Nicolson.

By the will of the Reichsführer SS [Heinrich Himmler], Auschwitz became the greatest human extermination center of all time.

When in the summer of 1941 he himself gave me the order to prepare installations at Auschwitz where mass exterminations could take place, and personally to carry out these exterminations, I did not have the slightest idea of their scale or consequences. It was certainly an extraordinary and monstrous order. Nevertheless the reasons behind the extermination program seemed to me right. I did not reflect on it at the time: I had been given an order, and I had to carry it out. Whether this mass extermination of the Jews was necessary or not was something on which I could not allow myself to form an opinion, for I lacked the necessary breadth of view.

Following Orders

If the Führer [Adolf Hitler] had himself given the order for the "final solution of the Jewish question," then, for a veteran National Socialist and even more so for an SS officer there could be no question of considering its merits. "The Führer commands, we follow" was never a mere phrase or slogan. It was meant in bitter earnest.

Since my arrest it has been said to me repeatedly that I could have disobeyed this order, and that I might even have assassinated Himmler. I do not believe that of all the thousands of SS officers there could have been found a single one capable of such a thought. It was completely impossible. Certainly many SS officers grumbled and complained about some of the harsh orders that came from the Riechsführer SS, but they nevertheless always carried them out.

Many orders of the Reichsführer SS deeply offended a great number of his SS officers, but I am perfectly certain that not a single one of them would have dared to raise a hand against him, or would have even contemplated doing so in his most secret thoughts. As Reichsführer SS, his person was inviolable. His basic orders, issued in the name of the Führer, were sacred. They brooked no consideration, no argument, no interpretation. They were carried out ruthlessly and regardless of consequences, even though these might well mean the death of the officer concerned, as happened to not a few SS officers during the war.

It was not for nothing that during training the self-sacrifice of the Japanese for their country and their emperor, who was also their god, was held up as a shining example to the SS.

SS training was not comparable to a university course which can have as little lasting effect on the students as water on a duck's back. It was on the contrary something that was deeply ingrained, and the Reichsführer SS knew very well what he could demand of his men.

But outsiders simply cannot understand that there was not a single SS officer who would disobey an order from the Reichsführer SS, far less consider getting rid of him because of the gruesomely hard nature of one such order.

What the Führer, or in our case his second-in-command, the Reichsführer SS, ordered was always right.

Democratic England also has a basic national concept: "My country, right or wrong!" and this is adhered to by every nationally conscious Englishman.

The Extermination of Russian Prisoners

Before the mass extermination of the Jews began, the Russian *politruks* and political commissars were liquidated in almost all the concentration camps during 1941 and 1942.

In accordance with a secret order issued by Hitler, these Russian *politruks* and political commissars were combed out of all the prisoner-of-war camps by special detachments from the Gestapo. When identified, they were transferred to the nearest concentration camp for liquidation. It was made known that these measures were taken because the Russians had been killing all German soldiers who were Party members or belonged to special sections of the NSDAP [Nazi party], especially members of the SS, and also because the political officials of the Red Army had been ordered, if taken prisoner, to create every kind of disturbance in the prisoner-of-war camps and their places of employment and to carry out sabotage wherever possible.

The political officials of the Red Army thus identified were brought to Auschwitz for liquidation. The first, smaller transports of them were executed by firing squads.

While I was away on duty, my deputy, Fritzsch, the commander of the protective custody camp, first tried gas for these killings. It was a preparation of prussic acid, called Cyclon B [Zyklon B], which was used in the camp as an insecticide and of which there was always a stock on hand. On my return, Fritzsch reported this to me, and the gas was used again for the next transport.

The Gassing

The gassing was carried out in the detention cell of block 11. Protected by a gas mask, I watched the killing myself. In the crowded cells death came instantaneously the moment the Cyclon B was thrown in. A short, almost smothered cry, and it was all over. During this first experience of gassing people, I did not fully realize what was happening, perhaps because I was too impressed by the whole procedure. I have a clearer recollection of the gassing of nine hundred Russians which took place shortly afterward in the old crematorium, since the use of block 11 for this purpose caused too much trouble. While the transport was detraining, holes were pierced in the earth and concrete ceiling of the mortuary. The Russians were ordered to undress in an anteroom; they then quietly entered the mortuary, for they had been told they were to be deloused. The whole transport exactly filled the mortuary to capacity. The doors were then sealed and the gas shaken down through the holes in the roof. I do not know how long this killing took. For a little while a humming sound could be heard. When the powder was thrown in, there were cries of "Gas!," then a great bellowing, and the trapped prisoners hurled themselves against both the doors. But the doors held. They were opened several hours later, so that the place might be aired. It was then that I saw, for the first time, gassed bodies in the mass.

It made me feel uncomfortable and I shuddered, although I had imagined that death by gassing would be worse than it was. I had always thought that the victims would experience a terrible choking sensation. But the bodies, without exception, showed no signs of convulsion. The doctors explained to me that the prussic acid had a paralyzing effect on the lungs, but its action was so quick and strong that death came before the convulsions could set in, and in this its effects differed from those produced by carbon monoxide or by a general oxygen deficiency.

A Bloodless Method

The killing of these Russian prisoners of war did not cause me much concern at the time. The order had been given, and I had to carry it out. I must even admit that this gassing set my mind at rest, for the mass extermination of the Jews was to start soon and at that time neither [Adolf] Eichmann [head of the Gestapo's department concerned with Jewish affairs] nor I was certain how these mass killings were to be carried out. It would be by gas, but we did not know which gas or how it was to be used. Now we had the gas, and we had established a procedure. I always shuddered at the prospect of carrying out exterminations by shooting, when I thought of the vast numbers concerned, and of the women and children. The shooting of hostages, and the group executions ordered by the Riechsführer SS or by the Reich Security Head Office had been enough for me. I was therefore relieved to think that we were to be spared all these blood baths, and that the victims too would be spared suffering until their last moment came. It was precisely this which had caused me the greatest concern when I had heard Eichmann's description of Jews being mown down [in Russia] by the Special Squads [the *Einsatzkommandos*] armed with machine guns and machine pistols. Many gruesome scenes are said to have taken place, people running away after being shot, the finishing off of the wounded and particularly of the women and children. Many members of the *Einsatzkommandos,* unable to endure wading through blood any longer, had committed suicide. Some had even gone mad. Most of the members of these *Kommandos* had to rely on alcohol when carrying out their horrible work. According to [Hans] Höfle's description, the men employed at [SS officer Odilo] Globocnik's extermination centers consumed amazing quantities of alcohol.

The Jews Arrive

In the spring of 1942 the first transports of Jews, all earmarked for extermination, arrived from Upper Silesia.

They were taken from the detraining platform to the "cottage"—to bunker I—across the meadows where later building site II was located. The transport was conducted by Aumeier and Palitzsch and some of the block leaders. They talked with the Jews about general topics, inquiring concerning their qualifications and trades, with a view to misleading them. On arrival at the "cottage," they were told to undress. At first they went calmly into the rooms where they were supposed to be disinfected. But some of them showed signs of alarm, and spoke of death by suffocation and of annihilation. A sort of panic set in at once. Immediately all the Jews still outside were pushed into the chambers, and the doors were screwed shut. With subsequent transports the difficult individuals were picked out early and most carefully supervised. At the first signs of unrest, those responsible were unobtrusively led behind the building and killed with a small-caliber gun, that was inaudible to the others. The presence and calm behavior of the Special Detachment [the *Sonderkommando*, consisting of prisoners] served to reassure those who were worried or who suspected what was about to happen. A further calming effect was obtained by members of the Special Detachment accompanying them into the rooms and remaining with them until the last moment, while an SS man also stood in the doorway until the end.

It was most important that the whole business of arriving and undressing should take place in an atmosphere of the greatest possible calm. People reluctant to take off their clothes had to be helped by those of their companions who had already undressed, or by men of the Special Detachment.

The refractory ones were calmed down and encouraged to undress. The prisoners of the Special Detachment also saw to it that the process of undressing was carried out quickly, so that the victims would have little time to wonder what was happening.

A Calming Influence

The eager help given by the Special Detachment in encouraging them to undress and in conducting them into the gas chambers was most remarkable. I have never known, nor heard, of any of its members giving these people who were about to be gassed the slightest hint of what lay ahead of them. On the contrary, they did everything in their power to deceive them and particularly to pacify the suspicious ones. Though they might refuse to believe the SS men, they had complete faith in these members of their own race, and to reassure them and keep them calm the Special Detachments therefore always consisted of Jews who themselves came from the same districts as did the people on whom a particular action was to be carried out.

They would talk about life in the camp, and most of them asked for news of friends or relations who had arrived in earlier transports. It was interesting to hear the lies that the Special Detachment told them with such conviction, and to see the emphatic gestures with which they underlined them.

Many of the women hid their babies among the piles of clothing. The men of the Special Detachment were particularly on the lookout for this, and would speak words of encouragement to the woman until they had persuaded her to take the child with her. The women believed that the disinfectant might be bad for their smaller children, hence their efforts to conceal them.

The smaller children usually cried because of the strangeness of being undressed in this fashion, but when their mothers or members of the Special Detachment comforted them, they became calm and entered the gas chambers, playing or joking with one another and carrying their toys.

Some Knew Their Fate

I noticed that women who either guessed or knew what awaited them nevertheless found the courage to joke with the children to encourage them, despite the mortal terror visible in their own eyes.

One woman approached me as she walked past and, pointing to her four children who were manfully helping the smallest ones over the rough ground, whispered:

"How can you bring yourself to kill such beautiful, darling children? Have you no heart at all?"

One old man, as he passed by me, hissed:

"Germany will pay a heavy penance for this mass murder of the Jews."

His eyes glowed with hatred as he said this. Nevertheless he walked calmly into the gas chamber, without worrying about the others.

One young woman caught my attention particularly as she ran busily hither and thither, helping the smallest children and the old women to undress. During the selection she had had two small children with her, and her agitated behavior and appearance had brought her to my notice at once. She did not look in the least like a Jewess. Now her children were no longer with her. She waited until the end, helping the women who were not undressed and who had several children with them, encouraging them and calming the children. She went with the very last ones into the gas chamber. Standing in the doorway, she said:

"I knew all the time that we were being brought to Auschwitz to be gassed. When the selection took place I avoided being put with the able-bodied ones, as I wished to look after the children. I wanted to go through it all, fully conscious of what was happening. I hope that it will be quick. Goodbye!"

Shattering Scenes

From time to time women would suddenly give the most terrible shrieks while undressing, or tear their hair, or scream like maniacs. These were immediately led away behind the building and shot in the back of the neck with a small-caliber weapon.

It sometimes happened that, as the men of the Special Detachment left the gas chamber, the women would suddenly realize what was happening, and would call down every imaginable curse upon our heads.

I remember, too, a woman who tried to throw her children out of the gas chamber, just as the door was closing. Weeping, she called out:

"At least let my precious children live."

There were many such shattering scenes, which affected all who witnessed them.

During the spring of 1942 hundreds of vigorous men and women walked all unsuspecting to their death in the gas chambers, under the blossom-laden fruit trees of the "cottage" orchard. This picture of death in the midst of life remains with me to this day.

The Selection

The process of selection, which took place on the unloading platforms, was in itself rich in incident.

The breaking up of families, and the separation of the men from the women and children, caused much agitation and spread anxiety throughout the whole transport. This was increased by the further separation from the others of those capable of work. Families wished at all costs to remain together. Those who had been selected ran back to rejoin their relations. Mothers with children tried to join their husbands, or old people attempted to find those of their children who had been selected for work, and who had been led away.

Often the confusion was so great that the selections had to be begun all over again. The limited area of standing room did not permit better sorting arrangements. All attempts to pacify these agitated mobs were useless. It was often necessary to use force to restore order.

No Solidarity

As I have already frequently said, the Jews have strongly developed family feelings. They stick together like limpets. Nevertheless, according to my observations, they lack solidarity. One would have thought that in a situation such as this they would inevitably help and protect one another. But no, quite the contrary. I have often known and heard of Jews, particularly those from Western Europe, who revealed the addresses of those members of their race still in hiding.

One woman, already in the gas chamber, shouted out to a noncommissioned officer the address of a Jewish family. A man who, to judge by his clothes and deportment, appeared to be of very good standing gave me, while actually undressing, a piece of paper on which was a list of the addresses of Dutch families who were hiding Jews.

I do not know what induced the Jews to give such information. Was it for reasons of personal revenge, or were they jealous that those others should survive?

The Special Detachment

The attitude of the men of the Special Detachment was also strange. They were all well aware that once the actions were completed they, too, would meet exactly the same fate as that suffered by these thousands of their own race, to whose destruction they had contributed so greatly. Yet the eagerness with which they carried out their duties never ceased to amaze me. Not only did they never divulge to the victims their impending fate, and were considerately helpful to them while they undressed, but they were also quite prepared to use violence on those who resisted. Then again, when it was a question of removing the troublemakers and holding them while they were shot, they would lead them out in such a way that the victims never saw the noncommissioned officer standing there with his gun ready, and he was able to place its muzzle against the back of their necks without their noticing it. It was the same story when they dealt with the sick and the invalids, who could not be taken into the gas chambers. And it was all done in such a matter-of-course manner that they might themselves have been the exterminators.

Then the bodies had to be taken from the gas chambers, and after the gold teeth had been extracted, and the hair cut off, they had to be dragged to the pits or to the crematoria. Then the fires in the pits had to be stoked, the surplus fat drained off, and the mountain of burning corpses constantly turned over so that the draught might fan the flames.

They carried out all these tasks with a callous indifference as though it were all part of an ordinary day's work. While they dragged the corpses about, they ate or they smoked. They did not stop eating even when engaged on the grisly job of burning corpses which had been lying for some time in mass graves.

An Unsolved Riddle

It happened repeatedly that Jews of the Special Detachment would come upon the bodies of close relatives among the corpses, and even among the living as they entered the gas chambers. They were obviously affected by this, but it never led to any incident.

I myself saw a case of this sort. Once when bodies were being carried from a gas chamber to the fire pit, a man of the Special Detachment suddenly stopped and stood for a moment as though rooted to the spot. Then he continued to drag out a body with his comrades. I asked the Capo what was up. He explained that the corpse was that of the Jew's wife. I watched him for a while, but noticed nothing peculiar in his behavior. He continued to drag corpses along, just as he had done before. When I visited the Detachment a little later, he was sitting with the others and eating, as though nothing had happened. Was he really able to hide his emotions so completely, or had he become too brutalized to care even about this?

Where did the Jews of the Special Detachment derive the strength to carry on night and day with their grisly work? Did they hope that some whim of fortune might at the last moment snatch them from the jaws of death? Or had they become so dulled by the accumulation of horror that they were no longer capable even of ending their own lives and thus escaping from this "existence"?

I have certainly watched them closely enough, but I have never really been able to get to the bottom of their behavior.

The Jews' way of living and of dying was a true riddle that I never managed to solve.

All Were Affected

All these experiences and incidents which I have described could be multiplied many times over. They are excerpts only, taken from the whole vast business of the extermination, sidelights as it were.

This mass extermination, with all its attendant circumstances, did not, as I know, fail to affect those who took a part in it. With very few exceptions, nearly all of those detailed to do this monstrous "work," this "service," and who, like myself, have given sufficient thought to the matter, have been deeply marked by these events.

Many of the men involved approached me as I went my rounds through the extermination buildings, and poured out their anxieties and impressions to me, in the hope that I could allay them.

Again and again during these confidential conversations

I was asked: is it necessary that we do all this? Is it necessary that hundreds of thousands of women and children be destroyed? And I, who in my innermost being had on countless occasions asked myself exactly this question, could only fob them off and attempt to console them by repeating that it was done on Hitler's order. I had to tell them that this extermination of Jewry had to be, so that Germany and our posterity might be freed forever from their relentless adversaries.

There was no doubt in the mind of any of us that Hitler's order had to be obeyed regardless, and that it was the duty of the SS to carry it out.

An Eyewitness Account of a Gassing

Kurt Gerstein

Not all executions by gas were performed in gas chambers. The first attempts at gassing victims took place in the back of vans that had been specially modified. Some vans had the exhaust pipes altered so that the victims were poisoned by carbon monoxide gas. Other vehicles were modified so that poison gas, such as prussic acid (also known as Zyklon-B), could be dropped into the back of the vans where the victims were confined.

The following selection is an account of a bungled gassing at Belzec in 1942 by Kurt Gerstein, a spy in the SS. He had been imprisoned in 1938 in a concentration camp by the Nazis. When he learned his sister-in-law had been murdered by the Nazis, he joined the SS in 1941 in order to witness, sabotage, and report on its activities. He gave written statements about the extermination of the Jews to the Swedish government and attempted to give a report to the Papal delegate in Berlin. In this statement, Gerstein gives a factual account of the gassing in which hundreds of Jews were confined in a gas chamber for nearly three hours before the Germans could start a diesel engine whose exhaust would be used to kill the victims.

In January, 1942 I was named chief of the Waffen-SS technical disinfection services, including a section for extremely toxic gases.

From Kurt Gerstein, as quoted by Leon Poliakov in *Harvest of Hate* (New York: Walden Press, 1979). Copyright © 1979 by Leon Poliakov. Reprinted by permission of the American Jewish Committee.

On June 8, 1942, SS *Sturmführer* Günther of the RSHA [Reich Security Main Office] came to see me. He was dressed in civilian clothing. I had never met him before. He ordered me to get for him immediately 100 kilograms of prussic acid and to bring it to a place known only to the truck driver. He said he needed the acid for a top secret mission.

Several weeks later, we left for Prague. I had a vague idea of the purpose for which the prussic acid was going to be used, and what sort of an order I had been given, but I agreed to do it, because this was my long-awaited chance to see for myself what was going on. Besides, as an expert on prussic acid, my authority and competence were such that it would be easy for me, under some pretext, to say that the prussic acid was unusable, that it was spoiled, or something to that order, and so to prevent it being used for extermination purposes. We took along, pretty much by chance, Professor Pfannenstiel, a doctor of medicine with the rank of SS *Obersturmbannführer,* who was professor of hygiene at the University of Marburg on the Lahn.

As soon as the truck was loaded, we left for Lublin (Poland). There, SS *Gruppenführer* Odilo Globocnik was waiting for us. At the Collin plant, I expressly let it be understood that the acid was intended for use in killing human beings. That afternoon, one man showed a great deal of interest in our truck. As soon as he realized that he was being watched, he made a quick getaway. Globocnik said to us, "This is one of the most secret matters there are, even the most secret. Anyone who talks about it will be shot immediately. Only yesterday two who talked were shot." Then he explained to us: "At the present time—it was August 17, 1942—there are three installations:

1) Belzec, on the Lublin-Lwow road. A maximum of 15,000 people per day.
2) Sobibor (I don't know exactly where it is), 20,000 people a day.

3) Treblinka, 120 kilometers NNE of Warsaw.
4) Maidanek, near Lublin (under construction)."

Globocnik said: "You will have to disinfect large piles of clothing coming from Jews, Poles, Czechs, etc. Your other duty will be to improve the workings of our gas chambers, which operate on the exhaust from a Diesel engine. We need a more toxic and faster working gas, something like prussic acid. The Führer and Himmler—they were here the day before yesterday, August 15—ordered me to accompany anybody who has to see the installation." Professor Pfannenstiel asked him: "But what does the Führer say?" Globocnik answered: "The Führer has ordered more speed. Dr. Herbert Lindner, who was here yesterday, asked me, 'Wouldn't it be more prudent to burn the bodies instead of burying them? Another generation might take a different view of these things.' I answered: 'Gentlemen, if there is ever a generation after us so cowardly, so soft, that it would not understand our work as good and necessary, then, gentlemen, National Socialism will have been for nothing. On the contrary, we should bury bronze tablets saying that it was we, we who had the courage to carry out this gigantic task!' Then the Führer said: 'Yes, my brave Globocnik, you are quite right.' "

The next day we left for Belzec. Globocnik introduced me to SS [Wirth?] who took me around the plant. We saw no dead bodies that day, but a pestilential odor hung over the whole area. Alongside the station there was a "dressing" hut with a window for "valuables." Further on, a room with a hundred chairs, [designated as] "the barber." Then a corridor 150 meters long in the open air, barbed wire on both sides, with signs: "To the baths and inhalants." In front of us a building like a bath house; to the left and right, large concrete pots of geraniums or other flowers. On the roof, the Star of David. On the building a sign: "Heckenholt Foundation."

The following morning, a little before seven there was an announcement: "The first train will arrive in ten minutes!"

A few minutes later a train arrived from Lemberg: 45 cars with more than 6,000 people. Two hundred Ukrainians assigned to this work flung open the doors and drove the Jews out of the cars with leather whips. A loud speaker gave instructions: "Strip, even artificial limbs and glasses. Hand all money and valuables in at the 'valuables window.' Women and young girls are to have their hair cut in the 'barber's hut.' " (An SS Unterführer told me: "From that they make something special for submarine crews.")

Then the march began. Barbed wire on both sides, in the rear two dozen Ukrainians with rifles. They drew near. Wirth and I found ourselves in front of the death chambers. Stark naked men, women, children, and cripples passed by. A tall SS man in the corner called to the unfortunates in a loud minister's voice: "Nothing is going to hurt you! Just breathe deep and it will strengthen your lungs. It's a way to prevent contagious diseases. It's a good disinfectant!" They asked him what was going to happen and he answered: "The men will have to work, build houses and streets. The women won't have to do that, they will be busy with the housework and the kitchen." This was the last hope for some of these poor people, enough to make them march toward the death chambers without resistance. The majority knew everything; the smell betrayed it! They climbed a little wooden stairs and entered the death chambers, most of them silently, pushed by those behind them. A Jewess of about forty with eyes like fire cursed the murderers; she disappeared into the gas chambers after being struck several times by Captain Wirth's whip. Many prayed; others asked: "Who will give us the water before we die?" [A Jewish rite] SS men pushed the men into the chambers. "Fill it up," Wirth ordered; 700–800 people in 93 square meters. The doors closed. Then I understood the reason for the "Heckenholt" sign. Heckenholt was the driver of the Diesel, whose exhaust was to kill these poor unfortunates. SS Unterscharführer Heckenholt tried to start the motor. It wouldn't start! Captain Wirth came up. You could see he was afraid because I was there to see the disaster. Yes, I saw everything and waited. My stopwatch clocked it all: 50 minutes, 70 minutes, and the Diesel still would not start! The men were waiting in the gas chambers. You could hear them weeping "as though in a synagogue," said Professor Pfannenstiel, his eyes glued to the window in the wooden door. Captain Wirth, furious, struck with his whip the Ukrainian who helped Heckenholt.

Kill Them in a More Decent Way

Children, despite their youth and innocence, were not spared from being murdered in Adolf Hitler's Final Solution. Many survivors of the Holocaust have described the brutal ways in which the Nazis and their allies killed Jewish and other children. In this excerpt, Ernst Göbel, a German SS officer, relates one incident he witnessed in which young children were killed by other SS officers.

The victims were shot by the firing-squad with carbines, mostly by shots in the back of the head, from a distance of one metre on my command. Before every salvo Täubner gave me the order—'Get set, fire!' I just relayed Täubner's command. The way this happened was that I gave the command 'Aim! Fire!' to the members of the firing-squad, and then there was a crack of gunfire. Meanwhile Rottenführer Abraham shot the children with a pistol. There were about five of them. These were children whom I would think were aged between two and six years. The way Abraham killed the children was brutal. He got hold of some of the children by the hair, lifted them up from the ground, shot them through the back of their heads and then threw them into the grave. After a while I just could not watch this any more and I told him to stop. What I meant was he should not lift the children up by the hair, he should kill them in a more decent way.

Ernst Göbel, "Kill Them in a More Decent Way," in *"The Good Old Days": The Holocaust as Seen by Its Perpetrators and Bystanders.* Ernst Klee, Willi Dressen, and Volker Riess, editors. Translated by Deborah Burnstone. New York: Konecky & Konecky, 1988.

The Diesel started up after 2 hours and 49 minutes, by my stopwatch. Twenty-five minutes passed. You could see through the window that many were already dead, for an electric light illuminated the interior of the room. All were dead after thirty-two minutes! Jewish workers on the other side opened the wooden doors. They had been promised their lives in return for doing this horrible work, plus a small percentage of the money and valuables collected. The men were still standing, like columns of stone, with no room to fall or lean. Even in death you could tell the families, all holding hands. It was difficult to separate them while emptying the rooms for the next batch. The bodies were tossed out, blue, wet with sweat and urine, the legs smeared with excrement and menstrual blood. Two dozen workers were busy checking mouths which they opened with iron hooks. "Gold to the left, no gold to the right." Others checked anus and genitals, looking for money, diamonds, gold, etc. Dentists knocked out gold teeth, bridges, and crowns, with hammers. Captain Wirth stood in the middle of them. He was in his element, and, showing me a big jam box filled with teeth, said, "See the weight of the gold! Just from yesterday and the day before! You can't imagine what we find every day, dollars, diamonds, gold! You'll see!" He took me over to a jeweler who was responsible for all the valuables. They also pointed out to me one of the heads of the big Berlin store Kaufhaus des Westens, and a little man whom they forced to play the violin, the chiefs of the Jewish workers' commandos. "He is a captain of the Imperial Austrian Army, Chevalier of the German Iron Cross," Wirth told me.

Then the bodies were thrown into big ditches near the gas chambers, about 100 by 20 by 12 meters. After a few days the bodies swelled and the whole mass rose up 2–3 yards because of the gas in the bodies. When the swelling went down several days later, the bodies matted down again. They told me that later they poured Diesel oil over the bodies and burned them on railroad ties to make them disappear.

A Sympathetic German

Christa M.

Although the majority of Germans approved of—or at least had no objections to—Adolf Hitler's plan to exterminate the Jews, there were some who were horrified by what had happened to the Jews. The following excerpt is by a German woman, who, when she was fifteen years old, came across Jewish prisoners during their evacuation from the concentration camp in Dachau in 1945. Christa M. says it was human compassion that made her give the emaciated prisoners all the cheese she had just received from a give-away program. School friends, and even her parents, however, berated her for her act of humanity.

Towards the end of the war, we're scared to death whether the Russians or the Americans would get there. We didn't know anything about the Americans, much. But we knew enough about the Russians, and we were scared to death. They were approaching from both sides. Of course, there weren't any more schooling because of the bombing. Food was becoming short. Even so, we didn't really suffer—well, it was getting really short because I stole then. I used to go in the fields and steal potatoes and sugar beets. And I herded some cows in exchange for bread here and there, some eggs. Because there was no more help. I mean the fields were going rotten, so we worked the fields, too. There was no more farm help. [They were] all in the war.

And my mother had heard that there was free cheese given away. So she said, "Tomorrow morning, you get your rucksack, and you go over there and get all the cheese you can put your hands on."

The town was bedlam, filled with SS, loudspeakers all over the place. Hitler screaming, I mean, like he screamed. I couldn't stand his voice. He always screamed and screamed, "We're winning the war!" You don't have to be very bright. You look around you and then you hear this, "We're winning the war," and you're in shambles.

Beyond Belief

I was walking east. There was a school [that] used to be used as a private girls' school, that had big walls surrounding the property. When I turned the corner, I saw—it's still, now, it's just hard for me because there are no words. There really are no words. There are no words. I can't find words. Well, there were people leaning against that wall, sort of hunched, quite a few, and there were some few standing in the middle of the street in little clumps. And they all had the blue and white striped uniforms. We had seen uniforms like that in the paper so I thought—I knew they were prisoners. But I didn't know what prisoners. But, my God, they are skeletons. I mean skeletons! I'll never forget the eyes. The eyes were three times the size because there were no more faces. Skeleton hands. And I see all these people. And the ones that were against the wall, they couldn't even walk. They could not walk, and so I immediately went towards them—I don't know, it was just a reaction. I really don't know what made me do it. Human compassion or whatever. I had food. These people, the first thing was these people must get food. And all I had was this cheese. So I started opening my rucksack, and the minute I reached in and got the first piece, these people came literally crawling. If you can imagine, people crawling, as much as they could, on hands and knees towards you. Just looked at you. To this day, I see those eyes. I see those faces. And just for the cheese.

So I gave the cheese out. I had almost given it all away, and a little bit left. And I feel like a bayonet in my back. It was an SS guy. And that's the first time I've really seen an SS guy close up, [with] the insignia on. He's got the big German shepherd. And he screamed at me—again, that screaming—"If you give those bastards one more piece of whatever you got there," he said, "I'm going to make you join them! You're going to go right with them!" And I started running. I got away from that guy.

They Shot Them!

I see the columns marching as far as I could see. . . . The people had wooden clogs on and rags around their feet, and they couldn't—their feet were bloody and they couldn't walk anymore. They were just shuffling, and it was drizzling and raining, and they didn't have any hats. I remember the little soup bowls, but I never saw anybody giving any soup out there at all. And they had them on their heads, and I thought, "Oh, my God. They're putting them on their heads because they don't want to get their heads wet." You know, you're a kid. Meantime it didn't occur to me that they didn't even have food. And the SS was pushing them and shoving them. And anytime, anytime somebody fell out of line—because they're exhausted, they couldn't walk—so anybody who could not keep in step, they shot them! I saw one directly in front of me. He fell. He could not move—he or she, I don't remember, I couldn't tell, they were all skeletons—and he let the dog loose. The dog went right for the jugular and he [the guard] just stood there, took his revolver. He just shot him. I'm standing there, I couldn't—just shot him. Then yelled for the others to move on. . . .

No Sympathy

A classmate of mine came up on his bike. I was so glad to see a familiar face. I went up to him, and by then I started crying. I couldn't stand it anymore. I was falling apart and I said, "What's going on?" I wanted to jump on the back of

his bike, to ride with him for comfort. I wanted to be close
with someone I knew. I was afraid of everybody. He barks
back at me, and he said, "You're such a stupid ass. Don't
you know what's going on?" I said, "No, I don't know
what's going on." He said, "Well, they're emptying Dachau.
Those are all the prisoners from Dachau. They're going to
march them into the mountains and they're going to shoot
them. They already shot twenty thousand. They're going to
shoot the rest—and they should have done it long ago." And
that did me in completely. He took off. And he was the one
who I thought I'd get some comfort [from]. I found out later
he was the son of an SS officer.

Some sort of small supply truck came by. They threw the
door open, and somebody in there motioned for me to come
in because I was crying so bad. So I think they felt sorry for
me. I don't know. I went in, and it turns out they were German soldiers who had taken off their uniforms and had put
on their fatigues or something, because people were then
stealing already civilian clothes. The biggest thing then was
to get rid of your uniforms so you don't get caught. He had
stuff on the truck and there was a tarp over it. I said, "What
have you got in the truck?" "Oh, it's stale army bread. We're
going to dump it to lighten the load because we're getting
out of here. We want to get into Switzerland as fast as we
can." So I knew they were deserters. I said, "You're going
to dump this bread? See this hunger out here? Can't we give
it away?" He just sort of shrugged his shoulders. But he
reached back, he brought a loaf and I sort of broke off some
and I handed it out the window. Oh, my God. A prisoner
way in the back, he just fell. And the others fell like domi-
noes. They just fell over each other to get to that piece of
bread. People were so desperate just to get that little piece
of bread.

"Don't Make Things Up"

I just ran home the rest of the way. I was in *fine* shape when
I walked in the house [*sarcastically*]. I tried to tell my

mother. Of course, if a child of mine had come home look-ing the way I did, I would have done it differently. But the first thing she said was, "Where is the cheese?" I could have hit her. I could have hit her. "I gave it away." Of course, she got so mad. "You and your stories! Here you go again! What'd you do now?" This whole line of questions. "There are people out there," I said. "They're not even people," I said, "They're skeletons!" "You are so full of it! Get to your room!" I tried to get her up then. I said, "Walk up there with me! I'll show you!" But she wouldn't go. "No, no!" She didn't believe me. "Don't make things up." And it wasn't till much later, when she saw pictures after the war. But it was never discussed. And she would never say anything.

Chapter 6

Liberation

Chapter Preface

Although the concentration camps were surrounded by barbed and electrified wire, minefields, guard dogs, watch towers, and guards armed with machine guns, a few prisoners did manage to escape. The best chance for escape was if prisoners were working outside the camp; some managed to slip away unnoticed when the guards' backs were turned. Organized attempts at escape were rare, but a few were successful. In 1943 and 1944, inmates in three camps—Treblinka, Auschwitz, and Sobibor—smuggled in weapons and explosives and staged three unrelated revolts against the guards. Although hundreds participated in each of the escape attempts, only a small percentage managed to slip beyond the fences and remain free. Most of the others were killed during the fighting or recaptured and executed by the Germans.

As the Allies forced the Germans to retreat in 1944 and 1945, the Germans began to close the camps closest to the front. In some camps, all remaining prisoners were killed before the Germans moved on; in others, the prisoners were forced to march hundreds of miles to camps in central Germany. The Nazis did not intend to leave behind any living witnesses who could tell the advancing Allied armies the truth about what happened in the camps. Those who could not keep up were simply shot by the guards and left on the road. These evacuations became known as the death marches.

The Russians were the first Allied force to liberate a camp. They came upon Majdanek on July 23, 1944, and could not believe what they found inside: many starving prisoners near death and warehouses filled with the clothing of those who had already perished. The Russians invited the International Red Cross to document the atrocities they found and they published photos of the camps' inmates, but the world community dismissed them as Russian propaganda. It was not until American and British troops entered Dachau and other camps in Germany that the world began to believe that the Nazis truly had murdered 6 million people in the camps.

Rebellion

Thomas Toivi Blatt

Not all Jews went quietly to their deaths in the gas chambers. In three different camps during the summer and fall of 1943, small groups of inmates rose up independently of each other in revolt against their guards. Although the guards crushed the rebellions, a few prisoners did manage to escape and elude recapture. Thomas Toivi Blatt is a Polish Jew who participated in the rebellion at Sobibor in eastern Poland on October 14, 1943. In the following account, Blatt relates how the Jews involved in the plot killed SS guards one by one, stealing their weapons, until their plan was discovered. From then on, it was open revolt. Of the three hundred Jews in the camp who managed to escape through the barbed wire fence and mine fields, Blatt is one of 150 who avoided recapture.

On October 14, 1943, the sun rose slowly over the horizon. It would be a warm day. SS Oberscharführer Bauer drove out to Chełm for supplies. The remaining Nazis in the camp went about their business as usual. Only a small group of Jews knew that this was to be a fateful day.

After the midday roll call, Kapo Pożycki, as planned, used his authority to take several conspirators—Sasha Pechersky, Siemion Rosenfeld, Boris Cybulski, Kali Mali, and Arkady Wajspapier—out of their normal work detachment and transfer them to Lager I. They assembled in the cabinetmaker's shop and set up headquarters.

At about 2:00 P.M., SS Unterscharführer Walter Ryba entered Lager I with a machine gun and took out four Jews,

Excerpted from *From the Ashes of Sobibor*, by Thomas Toivi Blatt. Copyright © 1997 by Northwestern University Press. Reprinted by permission of Northwestern University Press.

including Kapo Pożycki. Had there been a betrayal? A short time later Kapo Bunio arrived and reported that Pożycki and the others were taken to work in Lager IV, temporarily piling wood. The Nazi had been armed with a machine gun only because he had been the sole guard of these Jews.

The Stage Is Set

At precisely 4:00 P.M. the stage was set. Now everything depended on the nerve of the attackers, their faith in themselves, and a lot of luck. Since Commandant SS Reichleitner was absent, Untersturmführer Niemann was the acting commandant. He would be the first to be killed. Shubayev and Yehuda Lerner were waiting in the tailor shop in Lager I with their axes hidden.

A few minutes earlier than appointed, Niemann rode up on his beautiful white horse. Dreszer, the twelve-year-old putzer, ran up to hold the harness. Niemann entered the tailor shop. Mundek the tailor was ready, holding the new uniform. The German, without suspicion, unhooked his belt with its pistol in the holster and casually threw it on the table.

As tailors have done for ages, Mundek patted and turned Niemann at his will. Finally he told him to stand still while he marked the alterations with crayon. Then a terrible blow fell from behind. The Nazi dropped like a fallen tree, his head split.

Lerner stood for a second with the bloody ax in his hand, then struck again. Unexpectedly, the cap maker standing by broke down and began to stab the dead body hysterically with his scissors, calling out the names of his wife and children killed in Sobibor. When no one could quiet him, he was gagged and put in a closet. Niemann's body was taken to another room, and the bloody floor was cleaned with rags. The horse whinnied as if it sensed something wrong, and Dreszer took him to the stables. Shubayev rushed to Sasha's quarters to deliver the first pistol. There was now no turning back.

The Second Guard

In turn, SS Oberscharführer Siegfried Graetschus, the German then in charge of the Ukrainian guards, arrived at the cobbler shop to pick up his order. He was asked by Yitzhak Lichtman, the cobbler, to sit down and was helped to remove his boots so as to try on the new ones. While Yitzhak held the Nazi's leg in a firm grip, pulling off the boots, Wajspapier and Rosenfeld slipped out of the back room and split the skull of the Nazi with an ax. The cobblers barely had time to hide the body when his deputy, the Ukrainian Klatt, entered, calling the boss to the telephone. He was attacked by the same pair of conspirators and soon joined Graetschus on the floor, dead. Now, with their two prominent commanders dead, the Nazi staff was practically leaderless.

I prepared the incinerator building in Lager II in accordance with Leon's instructions days before. I shoved heaps of unburned documents against the window to obstruct the view.

A Change in Plans

Impatiently awaiting the arrival of the assassin group, I was looking through the open door. Suddenly I saw Kapo Bunio come in from Lager I with Cybulski, a thirty-five-year-old truck driver from Donbas, and another man I didn't know. I was surprised when the group went past the incinerator and continued toward the warehouses. Soon Sender, a tall Jew from Łódź, came to me and explained the last-minute change and the reason for it. The incinerator was too close to the fence and the guard towers. Even if the assassinations of the SS were successful there, the guard in the towers could become suspicious of the Germans' prolonged disappearance. Instead Sender ordered me to take up a position at the gate leading from Lager II to Lager I to prevent unauthorized persons from leaving their workplaces. If anyone were to ask me why, I was to say it was a German order.

This was a very sensitive area close to the warehouse where the killing of some Nazis was planned, and there were many people who could discover the plot and panic. I dug out from under the trash a beautiful, large, folded knife that I had hidden. It had a pearl-like handle and the Hebrew inscription *Kosher l'Pesach* (kosher for Passover), obviously a ritual item. There were many of them in the luggage of the Dutch transports. I opened the blade and pushed the knife under my belt. Next I dug up from my hiding place, under the documents waiting to be burned, the valuables I'd hidden in preparation for escape—a fortune in diamonds, gold, and paper money.

Luring the Nazis

While leaving for the assignment, I noticed in the yard a fourteen-year-old boy, Fibs, standing at attention before SS Unterscharführer Wolf, reporting to him that a brand-new leather coat, exactly his size, had been set aside for him in the men's warehouse. The short, dark-haired Unterscharführer took the bait and went without hesitation in the direction of the warehouse, disappearing inside the huge wooden barrack.

In one of the many partitions of the warehouse, a few "special" prisoners were stocking tied packages against the wall, each containing ten articles of clothing. The bait—the coat—lay to one side.

SS Wolf entered. "Attention!" barked Kapo Bunio. The slaves froze. "Help the Herr Unterscharführer with the coat!" ordered the Kapo.

An inmate fetched the coat and held it for the German. The Nazi put his arm into the sleeve, and in a split second the scenario changed. With a strike of the ax by Cybulski, the enemy fell. They finished him off with knives, and the lifeless body was hidden under piles of the victims' clothing. The blood on the floor was covered with sand. With this done, the executions in Lager II began. The trap awaited the next Nazi.

I took up my position at the gate opposite the warehouse. Soon a prisoner approached to pass the gate. When I stopped him, he started to argue with me. I saw Sender standing nearby and called to him for help. Sender took over, and I went to fetch other Nazis.

At this time the dumpcarts with the food rations were on their way to Lager III. I flagged down SS Scharführer Vallaster, the driver, and told him that SS Wolf needed him urgently. He was led to the same warehouse and killed there.

The motionless carts were standing on the rails near the warehouse, and I stuffed my pockets with canned food. My friend Karolek was amazed and said, "Toivi, you are pretty sure you will survive." I nodded my head in confirmation.

The communications were kept alive by inconspicuous young couriers. They reported to the staff of the organization on the progress in Lagers I and II. Perfect examples of German punctuality and order, most of the Nazis came at their appointed times for their rendezvous with death. Others were lured to the traps. So far everything was going according to plan.

A Slight Hitch

SS Beckmann was summoned to the warehouse. I observed him approaching. At the doorway of the huge barracks, he stopped, hesitated as if by intuition, then turned around, and, without a word, headed to the administration building, where he had his office.

After Sasha was notified about this hitch, a second emergency group—consisting of Leon Feldheldler, Chaim Engel, and Kapo Pożycki's younger brother—was ready to attack Beckmann. Beckmann's office was small, and he was alone. Still, it was necessary to take him by surprise. Pożycki's brother knocked on the door, asking permission to enter for some clarification. Permission granted, they entered. Expecting only one person, SS Beckmann seemed upset. In seconds the intruders went into action. Caught by surprise, it was too late for him to react. Pożycki immobilized him in a headlock, then Chaim plunged the knife into his chest several times. The blade slipped on the German's rib, cutting Chaim's left hand. The Nazi tried to regain control, and, although severely wounded, he managed to let out a loud scream for help before succumbing. Pożycki took his revolver. They left him slumped behind his desk. In the next office SS Scharführer Steubel was then killed.

Close to 5:00 P.M. Cybulski returned to Lager I and reported to Sasha the successful elimination of four SS men in Lager II: Wolf, Beckmann, Vallaster, and Steubel. Shubayev also reported the severing of the telephone line.

Back in the garrison area, SS Unterscharführer Ryba had entered the car garage by chance. The prisoners working there seized their opportunity: he was killed immediately. This worried the organization's leaders, because the garage was open, located in the administration area, and could be prematurely discovered.

Obtaining Rifles

Meanwhile, in Lager I, Szlomo Szmajzner picked up his stovepipes and headed for the guards' barracks. The Ukrainian guards were on duty with the working prisoners, and Szlomo hoped that the other Ukrainians, free of duty, were probably amusing themselves with the Polish prostitutes who came from nearby towns. They hung out in the barracks just outside the camp. Everybody knew that Szlomo was the tinsmith and often fixed roofs, stoves, and related problems, so he did not arouse any suspicion. He was scared but decisive. "Today is the day," he was heard to repeat to himself.

He put the pipes away and climbed onto the roof to check the chimney so as to establish his presence there as legitimate. Back in the barrack, he made sure that no Nazis were inside and then searched the squad leader's room. Szlomo saw a couple of machine guns hanging on the wall, but they were too big to conceal in the pipes. In the other room he noticed rifles and ammunition belts with only a few cartridges. Satisfied, he nervously tried to put the rifles into the stovepipe. Because of the unlocked rifle bolts, they didn't fit easily. For someone familiar with rifles, locking the bolts would have taken just seconds, but Szlomo was holding a rifle for the first time in his life. Not giving up, he managed to fit two rifles into the pipe and rolled it in a blanket, together with one more rifle. Carrying the blanket with the rifles over his shoulder, he casually, without incident, passed the Ukrainian guard at the gate of Lager I.

From the main tower came the sound of a bugle announcing the end of the day's work. Kapos now assembled their work groups in various parts of the camp and returned to Lager I in customary military fashion. Their marching songs in Yiddish, German, Polish, Dutch, Ukrainian, and Russian echoed far beyond the barbed wires of the Sobibor forest.

A Day Seemingly Like Any Other

It seemed like any other day. In the courtyard, unsuspecting prisoners were standing in line for their coffee and bread. Their life or death would be determined in a matter of minutes! The operation, prepared and executed in secrecy, had gone like clockwork so far. Except for a few, the overwhelming mass of inmates had no idea what had already been accomplished.

Unsuspectingly, SS Unterscharführer Friedrich Gaulstich entered the area. Keeping his cool, Szlomo Leitman immediately asked him to come to the newly built barrack where he was working because of some problem with the bunks. The Nazi took the bait, but the untrustworthy Kapo Schmidt followed them. Pożycki, having returned with his group from Lager IV, intervened. He casually approached Schmidt from behind and whispered into his ear, "Stay away, don't mix in." When this was reinforced with the point of a knife, Schmidt understood. From then on Schmidt was under observation. The moment SS Gaulstich entered the barrack, his fate was sealed; an assault group took care of him. On average, from 4:00 P.M. on, one German was killed every six minutes.

The door to the blacksmith's shop was wide open. I was waiting for Szlomo Szmajzner inside; a few Russian Jews were standing in a corner talking quietly. Then Szlomo entered with the load in his arms. He was sweating and breathing heavily. He opened the blanket, and out fell three rifles. Before the Russians grabbed them, he was able to secure one for himself. A young girl, Zelda Metz, slipped in and dropped on the bench some ammunition she had stolen while working in Lager IV. Sasha was there too, manipulating a German revolver. Soon Walter Schwarz dropped in and reported the sabotage of the electrical transformer.

At the same time, a frantic search for SS Frenzel was still going on. On Pechersky's order, Siemion Rosenfeld was still waiting for him in the carpentry shop with an ax, but Frenzel had disappeared. Critical minutes were passing, and he was still out of reach. He was one of the main executioners at Sobibor and very dangerous.

At 6:00 P.M., as was customary, the German staff would gather for the evening roll-call. At that crucial time, the surviving Nazis would notice the conspicuous absence of their cohorts and sound the alarm. Most of the Jews remained unaware of what was occurring around them. They were standing in line for more coffee, or were busy eating or washing their pots. It was now 5:30 P.M. On Sasha's orders, Pożycki blew his whistle for roll-call preparation. It was fifteen minutes early, but the Kapo's authority was never disputed. People began to assemble.

The News Spreads

Now the news spread like wildfire. While standing in formation, I noticed religious Jews returning to the barracks to get the prayer shawls they had hidden. They assembled near the kitchen, saying Kaddish, swaying back and forth. Seeing no hope for salvation, they said the prayer for the dead—for themselves. Believing that all was in the hands of Divine Providence, they resisted their oppressors by openly sanctifying God's commandments.

An elderly tailor twisted his fingers in desperation and walked back and forth, lamenting to himself, "What do we need this for? We could live for a few weeks more. Now this will be the end." A few young men were sitting on some building material near the barracks. I recognized a buddy of mine with a blanket on his shoulders. He had been ill for two days, so it was possible that they were a group of sick and weak Jews. It was obvious that they had decided to stay: they appeared resigned to their fate. Others were saying good-bye to their friends and were looking for suitable weapons. Then more and more inmates nervously congregated in the yard.

The Call to Arms

Sasha, trying to form a column to march the people to the main gate leading outside, according to the original plans, heard gunfire and understood that something had gone wrong. (SS Bauer had returned from Chełm. Discovering that SS Beckmann was dead, he started shooting at the two prisoners unloading his truck.) He decided to act immediately. He jumped up on a table, looked down, and made a short speech in Russian, his native language. His voice was clear and loud so that everybody could hear, but he spoke composedly and slowly. He informed the people that the majority of the Germans had been killed, that there was no return. A terrible war was ravaging the world, and each individual is part of that struggle. He reminded them of the power of his motherland, the Soviet Union, and promised that, dead or alive, we would be avenged, and so would the tragedy of all humanity. He repeated twice that if by some miracle one might survive, he should be a witness to this crime forever. He ended with a call: "Comrades forward! Death for the Fascists!!!"

The guns in the towers remained silent. The guards probably thought that the nervous activity was normal. Before a roll call, the slightest shortcomings were heavily punished. And they were too far away to hear what was being said.

The mass of prisoners, coming from most of the nations of Europe and speaking diverse languages, now understood. From the assembled Jews, all of a sudden, a single, strange, and impatient voice was heard. *"FORWARD! HURRAH! HURRAH!"* It was quickly picked up, and, in a flash, the entire camp answered the call to defiance. Most of the Jews spontaneously divided themselves into two groups. A smaller group stormed the fences in Lager I, frantically cutting the barbed wires with axes and shovels, without concern for the ditch full of water and the mines. Some threw planks of wood to detonate the mines. The second, larger group, armed with an assortment of weapons, pushed its way forward toward the exit of Lager I to reach the main gate.

At that moment, a guard commander, the Volksdeutscher Schreiber, was riding his bicycle through the same exit. Not understanding what had happened, he yelled "Why are you pushing like cattle? Get in line!" When he understood, it was too late. He was immediately surrounded, thrown from his bike, and knifed. His pistol was confiscated. Not far away, I saw another guard in visible shock, continuously turning himself around as if set in motion, his outstretched hand still holding his rifle.

Others Join In

Another group of fifty prisoners, mostly Russian Jews under the escort of SS Scharführer Wendland and Ukrainian guards, were returning late from their construction work in Lager IV when shooting was heard. Seeing prisoners on the run, they instantly became aware of the revolt. They threw themselves on their guards, initially overpowering them, but then were showered with bullets from the tower. Most fell, but a few prisoners, with their work tools—shovels, saws, and axes—and their killed escorts' rifles in hand, ran to the gate and joined in the attack on the armory, which was then in progress.

In the armory, there were only a few complete rifles available to the Jews. Most were disassembled for cleaning. SS Dubois, in charge of the armory, was hit with an ax. While trying to run away, he was shot in the chest. The prisoners grabbed whatever weapons they could and hurriedly left to join the fight.

The Germans React

Not worrying about the gunfire, I was running forward. To my right I saw SS Wendland standing flat against the wall of the canteen. Slowly retreating to hide behind the corner, he sprayed the running prisoners with fire.

I also saw SS Frenzel reappear on the scene with his machine gun. He, together with SS Bauer, mobilized the stunned Ukrainian guards. They effectively blocked the passage to the main gate, where many of the prisoners were being killed. I could hear the bullets whistle by me. I saw a friend fall in front of me, then others.

The frontline Jews fell back for a few minutes. I stopped, my long knife of no use to me now, and backed off about fifty feet, then headed to the right of the Germans' quarters as a new wave of determined fighters, in a suicidal thrust, pushed forward again toward the main gate. A small group, including Sasha, Szlomo, Sender, myself, and another man with an ax, ended up between the fences in the peripheral guards' corridor. In the confusion, we had run into the entrance of this corridor, and in this way we did not have to pass the two barbed-wire fences and ditch; they were already behind us. Ahead of me lay only one more barbed-wire fence and fifteen meters of minefield. I stopped. Someone was trying to cut an opening in the fence with a shovel. Sasha, armed with a pistol, stood waiting, as did Sender and myself, both with knives in hand. Only Szlomo Szmajzner, calmly shooting his rifle, was able to silence the guard in the tower. I still remember marveling at his composure. Within minutes, more Jews arrived.

The Minefield

Not waiting in line to go through the opening under the hail of fire, they climbed the fence. Though we had planned to detonate the mines with bricks and wood, most of us did not do it; we couldn't wait. We preferred sudden death to a moment more in that hell. People were scrambling for freedom. When I was only halfway through the fence it crumbled and fell on top of me. I thought this was the end for me. Instead, this probably saved my life, for lying under the wires, trampled by the stampeding crowd, I saw mines exploding and bodies torn. And I realized, had I been able to get through earlier, I would have been killed with them.

Corpses were everywhere. The noise of rifles, exploding mines, grenades, and the chatter of machine guns assaulted my ears. The Nazis kept their distance while shooting at us, and we had only primitive knives and hatchets. The wave of escapees finally passed over me. Now I was alone, lying amid bodies. I tried to extricate myself, but it was difficult. The wire barbs were deeply imbedded in the thickness of my leather coat, taken at the last minute from the warehouse. This managed to trap me under the fence. I thought to myself: "Is this the end? I don't want to die!" Suddenly I had a flash of insight, and then it was relatively easy: I simply slid out from under my coat and left it tangled there. I ran through the exploded minefield holes, jumped over a single wire marking the end of the minefields, and I was outside the camp. Now to make it to the woods ahead of me.

It was so close. . . . I was behind the last of the fugitives. I went down a few times, each time thinking I was hit. Each time I got up and ran farther . . . one hundred yards . . . fifty yards . . . twenty more yards . . . and at last the forest. Behind us, blood and ashes. In the grayness of the approaching evening, the tower's machine guns shot down their last victims. The thirty Jews from Lager III, still unaware, were left behind.

The Death March

Jack Eisner

With the Russians closing in on the concentration camps in
Poland in the winter of 1944–45, the Germans began to evacuate the camps and erase all signs of the crimes that had occurred there. Records were burned, and in some cases, the
camps themselves were destroyed. Prisoners who could not
walk were executed; those who could still walk were
marched for days in the snow with little protection from the
cold. Of the sixty thousand prisoners who left Auschwitz in
January 1945, 25 percent died from starvation, cold, exhaustion, and murder before they reached the camps in Buchenwald, Dachau, and Mauthausen.

In April 1945, when British and American troops began to
invade Germany, the Germans repeated the evacuations, forc-
ing inmates from camps near Germany's borders to march to
camps in central Germany. Jack Eisner was a political prisoner at the Flossenburg concentration camp when the Germans force-marched the inmates toward Dachau. He writes
that, as with the earlier marches, inmates who could not keep
up were shot by guards and left along the roadside. Half of the
five thousand inmates who left Flossenburg with Eisner were
still alive on the fourth day of the march when they were liberated from their German captors by American troops.

As soon as the condemned Jews had passed through the
gates [of Flossenburg], the remainder of us began to
worry about what would happen next. There was no work.
The Messerschmitt plant had been abandoned and blown up.
The girls at the bordello had disappeared. Hunger became

extreme. We, the slaves, subsisted on only a watery soup and some grain. Even the "elite" began to run out of food.

Then, suddenly, after about a week, instructions came from the beleaguered SS chiefs in Berlin. Flossenburg's remaining inmates were to be marched some 250 kilometers south to Dachau, deep in the Bavarian hinterland, a new enclave.

Pandemonium

Pandemonium broke loose as the hungry masses heard of evacuation. They did not want to follow the path of the Jews. Suddenly, in midmorning, hundreds of desperate inmates began an assault on the kitchen and its storage rooms. They blasted open all the doors, barrels, chests, and sacks, grabbing with both hands all they could manage. They stuffed their mouths, their pockets, and their shirts with potatoes, carrots, grain, and bread.

The entire episode lasted only minutes. The SS with their dogs rolled in on half-tracks, machine-gunning right and left. The dogs went wild.

The desperados did not care. They did not give up. Despite the hail of bullets and rivers of blood around them, they continued scrounging blindly, frantically, for food. When it was over, several hundred dead and wounded lay unattended. Several hours later, all the remaining prisoners were ordered to the *Appelplatz.*

The Death March

I was in a huge column of some 5,000 *Häftlinge,* the previously privileged prisoners. A few of the other hidden Jews—Sasha; and Romek and Leon, the musicians—were nearby. We were all marched to the gate in rows of five. Several SS guards with sacks of grain were stationed there on either side. They were passing out one handful to each inmate. This was to be the total provision for the march to Dachau. This was to sustain us while covering sixty to seventy kilometers a day—or night, since after that day, we were to march only at night.

Our pace was steady and uninterrupted—at least twelve hours of marching with no rest, additional food, or water. That torture soon began taking its toll. Prisoners by the hundreds began to slow down. Those unable to continue marching were shot by the SS, who were riding behind the column on motorcycles with machine guns mounted on sidecars.

I heard the gunfire clearly. It now became an almost continuous chain of staccato bursts. Anyone who fell, or attempted to sit down or rest, faced the same fate. Guards marching on both sides were constantly shooting. Pulling Sasha along with me, I pushed myself up ahead, as far from the executions as possible.

After the first night, we were herded together high on a hill, while the SS surrounded us from below. They were still concerned that no one escape. No one did. Everyone was too exhausted to move. A few were crawling around, looking for a cigarette butt or tobacco. They were offering their last remnants of grain for one puff. For three consecutive nights, our long column was driven through the dark side roads of Bavaria. Not a soul was to be seen. Even the villages we passed seemed deserted.

Exhaustion

After the second night of marching, I developed blisters on my feet. I removed my heavy wooden shoes and carried them on my back. Then I threw them away altogether. I also discarded my ragged blanket. On the third night, I disposed of my jacket and sweater, as well. I was walking in my bare feet, with a torn shirt and wet pants. I was even ready to shed them, too.

My sense of reality was fading. I was beginning to see rings around the moon and the stars. I was using all my will power not to faint. The last few weeks of skimpy food rations had radically reduced my weight. My body was no more than a bundle of bones held together by a sack of skin.

I Will Survive

Suddenly I felt a chill run through me as a vision of Pig's Corner flashed through my mind. No! I hadn't reached that stage yet. I wasn't a *Musulman* yet, a skeleton with a huge shaved head and big bulging eyes. A *Musulman* is apathetic and pain-free. His brain can no longer communicate with his body. It can no longer accept messages of fear or passion. His mind can only contemplate his own end. No! This is not me. Not yet. I can still feel pain and anger. I can still yearn for revenge. I can still survive.

Yes! I still wanted to survive. I felt this had to be my last great effort. That it would somehow be rewarded. I didn't know how. I couldn't predict anything. I just wanted to be the last Jew on earth. I wanted to march down on my final journey to the great exhibition hall of the World's Museum. Humanity would marvel at me, the survivor, who had managed the impossible. They would marvel at me, the last living specimen of 5,000 years of Jewish civilization. The Allies would bathe in the glory of their victory. The Third Reich would wallow in its ruins. But I, the survivor, would be condemned forever, neither able to rejoice nor to forget.

Machine-gun fire roused me from my reverie. The SS were shooting again. The column had to keep marching. I could see the SS in action. They were right behind me on their motorcycles. I urged myself onward. But the column continued to shrink. No longer caring, many inmates just sat down or tried to run. None made it. The SS gunned them down.

Karl the Stuttgarter, my ally for so long, tried to flee into the woods. But the SS shot him in front of me.

"This march will finish us all before we get to Dachau," I whispered to Sasha. "Only the SS will make it on their motorcycles. We'll go straight to heaven via a shortcut."

The Fourth Day

On the morning of the fourth day, April 23, Henry, the violinist, passed me, then slowed down again. He reached into his pockets and took out some leftover grain, a small knife, and a few other mementos. He handed them to his fellow musicians—Shlamek, Itzek, Yosek, and Heniek—and to me.

"Here, take this," he said. "Don't forget me if you make it. I can't go on. Let them finish me. How much can a human take?"

He started to slump to the side, but we all grabbed him and shouted, "Walk! Walk! Walk! You can't do this. We won't let you!"

We struggled with him, urging him to keep fighting. Finally, he was persuaded and continued to walk on his own. I returned his knife. "That's yours. Show it to me after it's all over."

The column was stopped for a rest on a small hill. The clear sky gave way to dark clouds; soon a heavy rain started to fall. But it didn't seem to bother the weary marchers. Exhausted, they fell to the ground and slept.

I climbed to the top of the hill to get as far away as possible from the trigger-happy guards below. On the way, I fell into a ditch of stagnant water. I crawled out, picked some grass and leaves for a pillow—enough to keep my head out of the mud—and fell asleep. I awoke to the sound of gunfire.

"*Du Sau!* You pig! Get back up there!" An SS man was kicking me. In my sleep, I had rolled all the way down the hill.

Still Alive

I got to my feet and started back up the hill. I could not see anything but steam. It was rising in thick clouds from the ground and the soaked inmates, who were lying there asleep. The rain poured down on us, but no one cared. Hundreds of inmates had rolled down the hill in their sleep. They felt nothing. Most of them lay wounded or dead, face down, shot in their sleep. They never knew what hit them. I managed to climb back up the hill, but I didn't fall asleep any more that morning.

At midday, the rain stopped, and the SS started to collect their gear and scream orders. *"Alles runter! Weiter marschieren!* Everyone march!" They fired their guns in the air to hurry us along.

The rain, which had trickled down my throat, had satisfied my thirst, but my hunger was indescribable. I had twisted my ankle as I rolled down the hill, so now I was walking with a limp. Soaked and barefoot, I was wearing only a pair of striped pants and the torn remnants of my shirt.

But I was still alive. Still alive, at two minutes to twelve. Still alive after six long years of horror and struggle. Would I make it? Would I ever know freedom again? I looked up at the sky as the sun's rays pushed past the clouds. I thanked nature for the sunshine. It warmed and soothed me, a mass of bone and will power.

We entered the town of Stamsried. Civilians and German soldiers were milling about the main square. The SS steered us away from the center of town, away from the civilians. But the civilians saw us, anyway. It made no difference. No one offered us food or hope in any form, even though we shouted and begged, "Bread! Water! Please!"

The SS squeezed us onto a side road. They shot anyone who moved too slowly. The sun was shining full force. The death march had cut the column to less than half its original length.

I dragged my body along. My strength was almost gone. Only my mind was urging me on. Only my will to survive. To see Halina. To watch the Third Reich collapse. My most cherished desires. Only they moved me forward. I lost sight of Sasha and the others. I didn't know whether they had fallen behind me, or I behind them.

Suddenly I heard a loud rumbling sound behind me. I watched in astonishment as the SS troops began to run for the woods. They were in absolute panic. They were riding their motorcycles across the open fields. They were abandoning guns and equipment.

Now a huge green monster of a tank came rumbling toward me. I jumped off the road into a ditch.

Liberated at Last

The tank passed me. Then another. And another. I could see stars painted on their sides. Soldiers in the turrets were firing their guns at the fleeing SS. Other soldiers were tossing packages on the road.

Frightened and bewildered, I just looked at the packages. Maybe they were bombs of some sort. Maybe they would explode. Then I heard someone shout. "Russians! *Zdrastvuytie tovarishche!*" That would account for the stars.

More tanks rumbled by. More packages rained down on us. I picked one up. I held it gingerly, turning it carefully in my hands. Then I read the lettering on the side: "U.S. Army—Ration C."

"America! American tanks!" I shouted at the top of my lungs.

The jubilant cry went up on all sides. "America! America! America!"

I opened my package and gulped its contents.

The tanks thundered by in an endless stream. I counted fifty, a hundred, even more. They passed for hours. Then artillery trucks appeared. Some of the trucks stopped, and the soldiers urged us in sign language to move back behind the lines. Other soldiers jumped from the trucks and ran into the woods after the SS men.

The rations had satisfied my hunger for the moment, so I started to walk in the direction the soldiers had indicated. Then it hit me: I was free! Liberated!

I suddenly became alarmed. Was it true? Was it real? Or was I dreaming? I didn't want to risk losing my precious freedom again. I wouldn't look for food and clothing now. I would walk and walk until I was sure I was safe.

The road was filled with an endless stream of American troops. "On to Berlin!" they were shouting. "On to Berlin!" Their words floated to my ears like sweet music. I loved these troops, these brave American soldiers. They were so beautiful to me. Germany was collapsing. The SS were on the run. And I was watching the whole fabulous show. I never believed I would live to see it. But now I was free and walking farther and farther away from the front lines. The other liberated slaves, hundreds of them, were searching for food in every farmhouse and barn along the way. I urged them to move back with me, but they wouldn't listen. All they wanted was food.

Food and Sleep

Finally, alone, I dragged myself back to the village of Stamsried. Gum-chewing American MPs were standing guard over groups of German POWs. Now and then, a trickle of slaves showed up in their striped uniforms. The GIs talked to us, offered us food, and tried to make us smile. They didn't know what to do to help us.

They led me to a house occupied by U.S. soldiers. I understood no English. In sign language, they urged me to take some clothing left behind by the Nazi owner.

The GIs threw a party with wine, Coca-Cola, and spaghetti. I had never tasted Coca-Cola. I was afraid to try it. My fear triggered some well-meaning laughs. Johnny, an Italian-American, offered me some spaghetti that I wolfed down from my cupped hands.

I felt tired and weak. I needed sleep. The Americans promptly obliged. They prepared a bedroom for me, a whole room all to myself. White sheets, pillows, blankets, pajamas. But I was afraid to sleep on such a clean, soft bed. I stared at it for a long time, then climbed out the window and sneaked down to the basement, where I stretched out comfortably on the floor.

I fell asleep with my hand in my pocket. A few grains were still there.

Liberation Day

Lucie Adelsberger

Lucie Adelsberger was a Jewish doctor in Auschwitz who was among the inmates who were evacuated to Ravensbrück concentration camp in northern Germany in the spring of 1945. She relates in the following essay how the camp inmates watched Allied and German planes battle in the air above them and heard the distant bombardment of guns for weeks without any apparent change in their situation. According to Adelsberger, the most difficult part of liberation was waiting for their liberators to actually arrive. The prisoners' hopes rose with every rumor and battle and fell when the rumors proved false. When the Allies finally arrived in their camp, they were greeted with jubilation. However, Adelsberger notes, among the feelings of joy were also feelings of emptiness. After so many years in captivity, she writes that the freed prisoners had to learn how to be free again.

One might expect the liberation to be the brightest chapter in the history of the concentration camp. That's not necessarily true, at least not without certain qualifications.

We'd been waiting for imminent liberation from early April [1945] on, and we experienced every high and every low point of this vigil with excruciating clarity. Since every high point had to be paid for with many low ones, our spirits were more down than up. Many things spoke in favor of an Allied advance: the countless American and Russian fighter plane squadrons that circled above the camp, the exciting air battles that were played out over our heads, and the muffled pounding of the distant guns that gradually grew louder and closer in the nocturnal stillness. But this went on for weeks, in a constant but not increasing barrage. We had recently been transported to Neustadt, a little town that didn't seem to exist on the map of Europe; wedged in between two fronts, it was apparently overlooked by both sides, and us with it. Even if they were to search us out— Red Cross packages actually did reach us on April 12th— the Germans would probably make good their threat to bombard at the very last moment, leveling the camp and us at the same time.

Waiting

The interminable waiting took its toll on our nerves. We had never been so impatient, not even through all the years with no hope of rescue. Veteran prisoners with overcompensating callousness became jumpy and irritable. Sleep was out of the question; we spent the nights straining our ears, listening in the void, noting every sound and registering the slightest oscillation and vibration in the immediate vicinity like a seismograph. Presentiments and nightmares produced rumors, and out of rumors developed chimeras that evaporated in thin air and hopes that burst like bubbles within a few hours.

On Monday, April 30th, we learned that the SS fighter pilot corps that was stationed all around our camp had been issued the following ultimatum: "The SS fighter pilot corps is summoned to surrender by 3 P.M. Tuesday afternoon and to land all planes at X on the other side of the Elbe." (We were never able to discover where X was.) We stood behind our wire fences, our eyes glued to every single movement the fighter pilots made; we were so excited we didn't even know whether the neighboring barracks had been evacuated or not.

Two days later—it was now May 2, 1945—the tension rose to a climax with the news that "Ravensbrück Concentration Camp, our main camp, has been liberated." We were familiar with this announcement, for it had been repeated at least fifty times and in every conceivable variation since the beginning of March. But this time it really was true. The women overseers who had fled the camp brought the news personally in the early morning hours, and toward nine o'clock the camp leader gave a dulcet speech in which he confirmed the fact. He said something about the prisoners being consigned to the care of the Swedish Red Cross. He promised under sacred oath that not a hair on our heads would be harmed and, what's more, that he'd protect us from all danger and personally hand us over to the beneficent custody of the Allied forces. That was in the morning.

The Aftereffects of Liberation

Life did not immediately return to normal for the inmates once the concentration camps were liberated by the Allies. For some, it took months just to look like a human being again. Others had no home or family to which they could return. Once freed, many former inmates became depressed. Psychiatrist Viktor E. Frankl discusses some of the other effect of liberation on the former prisoners.

When we spoke about attempts to give a man in camp mental courage, we said that he had to be shown something to look forward to in the future. He had to be reminded that life still waited for him, that a human being waited for his return. But after liberation? There were some men who found that no one awaited them. Woe to him who found that the person whose memory alone had given him courage in camp did not exist any more! Woe to him who, when the day of his dreams finally came, found it so different from all he had longed for! Perhaps he boarded a trolley, traveled out to the home which he had seen for years in his mind, and only in his mind, and pressed the bell, just as he has longed to do in thousands of dreams, only to find that the person who should open the door was not there, and would never be there again.

By the time afternoon came around he'd forgotten all his promises or at least considered them superfluous; more important seemed to be his own safety. By three o'clock the otherwise so noisy SS vanished quickly and quietly from the camp, without attracting any attention.

Liberation

At a quarter to four an American jeep manned by a forward patrol turned up. He was greeted with unbounded jubilation, almost smothered in exuberant embraces, and borne aloft on the shoulders of enthusiastic girls. In no time flat the jeep

---

We all said to each other in camp that there could be no earthly happiness which could compensate for all we had suffered. We were not hoping for happiness—it was not that which gave us courage and gave meaning to our suffering, our sacrifices and our dying. And yet we were not prepared for unhappiness. This disillusionment, which awaited not a small number of prisoners, was an experience which these men have found very hard to get over and which, for a psychiatrist, is also very difficult to help them overcome. But this must not be a discouragement to him; on the contrary, it should provide an added stimulus.

But for every one of the liberated prisoners, the day comes when, looking back on his camp experiences, he can no longer understand how he endured it all. As the day of his liberation eventually came, when everything seemed to him like a beautiful dream, so also the day comes when all his camp experiences seem to him nothing but a nightmare.

The crowning experience of all, for the homecoming man, is the wonderful feeling that, after all he has suffered, there is nothing he need fear any more—except his God.

Viktor E. Frankl, *Man's Search for Meaning.* New York: Washington Square Press, 1984.

was bedecked with green boughs. Half an hour later he drove off and was soon followed by the liberating Russians.

And then what? A free-for-all for the arriving care packages, riotous plundering of the SS storerooms and whatever belongings the overseers had left behind, a wild tumult, with screaming, weeping, laughing, handshakes, and hugs, and amidst all this exuberance—an empty void.

A years-old yearning, a hope we hardly dared express even in our dreams, had actually come true—it was something even the most fanciful among us could never have imagined. We were incredulous and dumbstruck that first hour, when this inconceivable, unfathomable good fortune descended upon us. It was overwhelming, and it shattered us. Just as our starving bodies at first refused to digest the food they were now offered, so, too, were we unable to completely absorb our new freedom in those first hours. We had to accustom ourselves to it first, and we faltered along with clumsy, hesitant steps into our newly won life.

Gradually, of course, we did comprehend it. If I were to describe how we strolled through the beechwood forest during those early days in May, uninhibited and unguarded, and how we gazed through the tops of the birch trees to the heavens beyond, the heavens we could once again call our own, or how I stood in front of a blooming Japanese cherry tree and stroked the forsythia bushes with hands unshackled, and wandered through meadows bounded not by wires but only by the horizon, alone, free, and yet still connected to the wide world—if I were to describe all that, I'd have to be a poet: The heavens had opened.

A War Correspondent's Story

Edward R. Murrow

Reports of the atrocities committed in the concentration camp
had filtered out to the free world via escapees and resistance
groups for several years before 1945, but many people refused to believe such horrible things could be happening. The
Russians distributed photographs of what they found when
they liberated the camps in Poland; however, much of the
world dismissed these reports as communist propaganda. It
was not until British and American troops arrived in the
camps in Germany in April 1945 that the world began to
comprehend the horror of Adolf Hitler's Final Solution.

Edward R. Murrow was a legendary reporter for CBS
News during World War II. The following selection is from
his newscast of April 15, 1945, in which he describes what
the liberators found when they entered the Buchenwald concentration camp in central Germany.

"Permit me to tell you what you would have seen and
heard had you been with me on Thursday. It will not
be pleasant listening. If you are at lunch or if you have no
appetite to hear what Germans have done, now is a good
time to switch off the radio, for I propose to tell you of
Buchenwald.

Reprinted from Edward R. Murrow's radio broadcast of April 15, 1945, as reprinted in
*The Liberation of the Nazi Concentration Camps, 1945: Eyewitness Accounts of the Lib-
erators*, edited by Brewster Chamberlin and Marcia Feldman (Washington, DC: U.S.
Holocaust Memorial Council, 1987).

"It is on a small hill about four miles outside Weimar, and it was one of the largest concentration camps in Germany. And it was built to last.

"As we approached it, we saw about nine hundred men in civilian clothes with rifles advancing in open order across the fields. There were a few shots. We stopped to inquire. We were told that some of the prisoners had a couple of SS men cornered in there. We drove on, reached the main gate. The prisoners crowded up behind the wire. We entered.

The Camp

"And now, let me tell this in the first person, for I was the least important person there, as you shall hear. There surged around me an evil-smelling horde; men and boys reached out to touch me. They were in rags and the remnants of uniforms. Death had already marked many of them, but they were smiling with their eyes.

"I looked out over that mass of men to the green fields beyond where well-fed Germans were plowing. A German, Fritz Kersheimer, came up and said, 'May I show you around the camp? I've been here 10 years.' An Englishman stood to attention saying, 'May I introduce myself? Delighted to see you. And can you tell me when some of our blokes will be along?' I told him, 'Soon,' and asked to see one of the barracks. It happened to be occupied by Czechoslovakians.

"When I entered, men crowded around, tried to lift me to their shoulders. They were too weak. Many of them could not get out of bed. I was told that this building had once stabled 80 horses; there were 1,200 men in it, five to a bunk. The stink was beyond all description.

"When I reached the center of the barracks, a man came up and said, 'You remember me; I'm Peter Zenkl, one-time mayor of Prague.' I remembered him but did not recognize him. . . .

"I asked how many men had died in that building during the last month. They called the doctor. We inspected his records. There were only names in the little black book, nothing more. Nothing of who these men were, what they had done or hoped. Behind the names of those who had died there was a cross. I counted them. They totaled 242—242 out of 1,200 in one month.

"As I walked down to the end of the barracks, there was applause from the men too weak to get out of bed. It sounded like the hand-clapping of babies, they were so weak.

"The doctor's name was Paul Heller. He had been there since '38. As we walked out into the courtyard, a man fell dead. Two others—they must have been over 60—were crawling towards the latrine. I saw it, but will not describe it.

"In another part of the camp they showed me the children, hundreds of them. Some were only six. One rolled up his sleeve, showed me his number. It was tattooed on his arm—D6030 it was. The others showed me their numbers. They will carry them till they die.

"An elderly man standing beside me said, 'The children—enemies of the state.' I could see their ribs through their thin shirts. The old man said, 'I am Professor Charles Richer of the Sorbonne.' The children clung to my hands and stared.

"We crossed to the courtyard. Men kept coming up to speak to me and to touch me—professors from Poland, doctors from Vienna, men from all Europe, men from the countries that made America.

The Hospital

"We went to the hospital; it was full. The doctor told me that 200 had died the day before. I asked the cause of death; he shrugged and said, 'Tuberculosis, starvation, fatigue, and there are many who have no desire to live. It is very difficult.' Dr. Heller pulled back the blankets from a man's feet to show me how swollen they were. The man was dead. Most of the patients could not move.

"As we left the hospital, I drew out a leather billfold, hoping that I had some money which would help those who lived to get home. Professor Richer from the Sorbonne said, 'I should be careful of my wallet, if I were you. You know there are criminals in this camp, too.'

"A small man tottered up saying, 'May I feel the leather, please? You see, I used to make good things of leather in Vienna.' Another man said, 'My name is Walter Roeder. For many years I lived in Joliet—came back to Germany for a visit, and Hitler grabbed me.'

"I asked to see the kitchen; it was clean. The German in charge had been a Communist, had been at Buchenwald for nine years, had a picture of his daughter in Hamburg—hadn't seen her for almost 12 years, and if I got to Hamburg would I look her up? He showed me the daily ration—one piece of brown bread about as thick as your thumb; on top of it a piece of margarine as big as three sticks of chewing gum. That and a little stew was what they received every 24 hours.

"He had a chart on the wall, very complicated it was. There were little red tabs scattered through it. He said that was to indicate each 10 men who died. He had to account for the rations. And he added, 'We are very efficient here.'

"We went again into the courtyard, and as we walked, we talked. The two doctors, the Frenchman and the Czech, agreed that about 6,000 had died during March. Kerscheimer, the German, added that back in the winter of '39, when the Poles began to arrive without winter clothing, they died at the rate of approximately 900 a day. Five different men asserted that Buchenwald was the best concentration camp in Germany. They had had some experience with the others.

The Crematorium

"Dr. Heller, the Czech, asked if I would care to see the crematorium. He said it wouldn't be very interesting because the Germans had run out of coke some days ago and had taken to dumping the bodies into a great hole nearby.

"Professor Richer said perhaps I would care to see the small courtyard. I said yes. He turned and told the children to stay behind.

"As we walked across the square, I noticed that the professor had a hole in his left shoe and a toe sticking out of the right one. He followed my eyes and said, 'I regret that I am so little presentable, but what can one do?'

"At that point, another Frenchman came up to announce that three of his fellow countrymen outside had killed three SS men and taken one prisoner. We proceeded to the small courtyard. The wall was about eight feet high; it adjoined what had been a stable or garage.

"We entered. It was floored with concrete. There were two rows of bodies stacked up like cordwood; they were thin and very white. Some of the bodies were terribly bruised, though there seemed to be little flesh to bruise. Some had been shot through the head, but they bled but little. All except two were naked. I tried to count them as best I could, and arrived at the conclusion that all that was mortal of more than 500 men and boys lay there in two neat piles.

"There was a German trailer which must have contained another 50, but it wasn't possible to count them. The clothing was piled in a heap against the wall. It appeared that most of the men and boys had died of starvation; they had not been executed. But the manner of death seemed unimportant—murder had been done at Buchenwald. God alone knows how many men and boys have died there during the last 12 years. Thursday I was told that there were more than 20,000 in the camp; there had been as many as 60,000. Where are they now?

"As I left that camp, a Frenchman who used to work for Havas in Paris came up to me and said, 'You will write something about this perhaps?' And he added, 'To write about this you must have been here at least two years. And after that, you don't want to write any more.'

"I pray you to believe what I have said about Buchenwald. I have reported what I saw and heard, but only part of it; for most of it I have no words. Dead men are plentiful in war, but the living dead, more than 20,000 of them in one camp—and the country . . . was pleasing to the eye, and the Germans were well fed and well dressed. American trucks were rolling toward the rear filled with prisoners. Soon they would be eating American rations—as much for a meal as the men at Buchenwald received in four days.

President Roosevelt

"If I have offended you by this rather mild account of Buchenwald, I am not in the least sorry. I was there on Thursday, and many men in many tongues blessed the name of Roosevelt. For long years his name had meant the full measure of their hope. These men, who had kept close company with death for many years, did not know that Mr. Roosevelt would within hours join their comrades who had laid their lives on the scales of freedom.

"Back in 1941, Mr. Churchill said to me, with tears in his eyes, 'One day the world and history will recognize and acknowledge what it owes to your President.' I saw and heard the first installment of that at Buchenwald on Thursday. It came from men from all over Europe. Their faces, with more flesh on them, might have been found anywhere at home. To them, the name Roosevelt was a symbol, a code word for a lot of guys named Joe who were somewhere out in the blue with the armor heading East.

"At Buchenwald they spoke of the President just before he died. If there be a better epitaph, history does not record it."

The Germans Share Collective Guilt

Benjamin Bender

When Allied troops confronted German and Polish civilians about the concentration camps which bordered their towns, most denied knowing anything about what happened inside the camps' fences. These denials infuriated the Allies and former prisoners alike, who questioned how anyone could not know what was happening. They maintained that the stench from the crematoria was enough by itself to let people know the truth about Adolf Hitler's Final Solution for the Jews.

In the following essay, Benjamin Bender has been released from Buchenwald and is traveling on a train where he meets a young German girl. Her father fought in the German army and she was a member of the Hitler Youth; yet she apologizes for what he endured. The German people share a collective guilt for the Holocaust, she asserts, and it is a stain that will remain on their conscience for ages.

After the liberation of Buchenwald, the Germans of Weimar swarmed to the camps en masse to witness the horrors of their insane leadership. Just in crushing defeat, the Germans came to sudden realization and awareness, claiming in shock a lack of information and deception. "We didn't know," some were crying in a sudden surge of emotions. They couldn't believe that these horrors were conducted next to their doors. Now they were traveling to Buchenwald back and forth, visiting a strange zoo, or a

From *Glimpses: Through Holocaust and Liberation*, by Benjamin Bender. Copyright © 1995 by Benjamin Bender. Reprinted with permission of North Atlantic Books, Berkeley, California, USA.

museum of an extinct human tribe. The picture they saw brought them many sleepless nights.

A Conversation

On the train I met a German girl, a teenager, long blond hair, blue eyes. She was first to introduce herself. "I am Rita Muller," she said politely.

I nodded my head, reluctant to talk.

"Are you from the camp?" She avoided mentioning the word Buchenwald.

"Yes I am from the camp," I answered nonchalantly.

"Is it true what we are being told about the Nazi atrocities?" She wanted first hand information.

"What you were told before by Adolf Hitler, your leader, was a lie, what you heard and saw now is true. The *Musulmans* [skeletal, corpselike figures] you saw used to be normal human beings," I answered icily.

She was pale, speechless.

"How old are you?" I asked, struggling to control my ire. My words came out rapidly. I didn't want to wait for a single answer. "What was your father doing during the war?" I continued.

"I am seventeen, my father was killed in Stalingrad, he was serving in the Wermacht," she answered defensively.

I didn't know whether to believe her. Every good German died in Stalingrad. At the "battle fields" of Treblinka and Auschwitz the Germans didn't die. I looked straight into her eyes. She challenged my look. She wasn't lying.

"What about you?" I continued to press. "I am sure you served in *Hitlerjugend* [Hitler Youth]."

"Yes, I was, I am not denying it, but I was in school. I didn't have a choice. In school we were obliged to undergo paramilitary service. I couldn't say no. They would punish me and throw me out of the school. At home my parents never taught me to hate, the hate came from outside. My father knew that the dream of a thousand year Third Reich would come to a bitter end. He was a soldier on the eastern front," she concluded in a firm voice.

"How can I believe you?" I said angrily. "I was working in Weimar, emaciated, starved to death. Your people were so aloof, indifferent. In the eyes of the Germans we were the *Untermensche* [subhumans], the damned slaves of the *Herrenvolk* [master race]. What makes people superior or inferior? We are born the same way and we die the same way. God doesn't discriminate, but the problem was that you didn't believe in God, you wanted to test him and you won, because the ruthless power rested with you," I concluded agitated.

Collective Guilt

She looked at me disoriented, defenseless. "I am not trying to defend Germany. Our guilt is collective, for knowing or not knowing. The people who inflicted on you this cruel sufferings were Germans. The gas chambers were German made. The idea of the final solution was German. You might not believe me, but I am ashamed to be German, because the stain on our conscience will remain for ages. Decent Germans could refuse the orders to kill, nothing would happen to them, the only punishment was to be sent to the Eastern front. They didn't do it because they were cowards. In no way can you forgive us. There is no way we can repent for the atrocities we have committed," she said, tears streaming down her face.

The train came to a screeching halt. She stretched out her hand, subdued, despondent. I looked at her, not knowing what to do next. She saw me hesitating but she kept her hand stretched out. I squeezed her hand, speechless, at a loss to utter a word. The Germans destroyed everything I had, my parents, grandparents and finally my only brother at the dawn of liberation. I couldn't look into her eyes, feeling that I committed blasphemy by betraying the sacred memory of my family. She was sobbing. When we parted she kept waving her hand.

Chronology

1933

January 30: Adolf Hitler becomes chancellor of Germany, beginning his persecution of the Jews.

March 20: The Nazis open Dachau, one of Germany's most notorious concentration camps. By July, more than twenty-five thousand political prisoners and Jews are in concentration camps around Germany.

April: The German Reichstag (parliament) passes several anti-Jewish laws, including laws prohibiting Jews from practicing law and working in the civil service; ordering Jewish government workers to retire; restricting Jewish children from enrolling in schools; and prohibiting Jews from practicing the ritual slaughter of animals for meat.

April 26: The Gestapo (Secret State Police) is established under the leadership of Hermann Göring.

1935

September 13: German Jews are stripped of their citizenship and rights by the Nuremberg Laws. Jews are also prohibited from marrying non-Jews.

1936

July 12: The Nazis round up German Gypsies and send them to the Dachau concentration camp.

1938

March 12: *Anschluss*—the German occupation of Austria. The next day, Hitler annexes Austria to Germany, adding two hundred thousand more Jews to the German Reich.

November 9–10: Jewish shops and nearly every synagogue in Germany and Austria are destroyed during *Kristallnacht* riots instigated by the SS. Thirty thousand Jews are arrested and sent to concentration camps.

1939

September 1: Germany invades Poland, starting World War II.

September 21: Polish Jews are ordered into ghettos. Their homes are seized by the German soldiers in order to resettle German families.

October: Hitler begins a euthanasia program of "undesirables" in Germany known as Operation T-4, and includes Jews in his order. Operation T-4 will kill seventy to eighty thousand people between 1939 and 1945, including the mentally and physically handicapped, the mentally ill, and Jews.

November 23: Polish Jews are ordered to wear a white band with a blue Star of David on it to publicly identify themselves.

1940

February 21: The Auschwitz concentration camp in Poland is established. Rudolf Höss, commandant of Auschwitz, estimates that 2 million Jews were gassed at Auschwitz, although it is subsequently shown that the figure is closer to 1.5 million.

October 12: The Warsaw ghetto is established. About five hundred thousand Jews are forced to live in an area of 3.5 square miles.

1941

June 22: Germany invades the Soviet Union. Special killing squads called *Einsatzgruppen* follow behind the German army and begin their mass murder of all the Jews, Gypsies, and Communist Party officials they can find.

July 21: The Majdanek concentration camp in Poland opens. Until its liberation in July 1944, over four hundred thousand people, mostly Jews, will die in this extermination camp.

September–October: Experiments at Auschwitz using the poisonous insecticide Zyklon-B find that it can be used to kill humans. A gaseous version of the poison will be used to kill millions of Jews.

October: Construction begins on an extermination camp known as Birkenau near Auschwitz. Germans begin tests using vans to gas victims.

November 1: Construction begins on the Belzec concentration camp. By the end of 1942, six hundred thousand Jews will be killed here.

December: The Chelmno death camp in Poland opens. The camp operated until March 1943. More than 150,000 Jews and 5,000 Gypsies will be murdered here.

December 7: Japan attacks Pearl Harbor, Hawaii, and the United States enters the war.

December 11: Germany declares war on the United States.

1942
February 15: The first mass gassing of Jews at Auschwitz-Birkenau begins.

March: The extermination camp at Sobibor in eastern Poland is nearly operational. Nearly two hundred fifty thousand Jews will be killed at this death camp before the Nazis order its demolition in November 1943.

June: The Treblinka death camp is founded. By mid-September, more than 250,000 Jews from the Warsaw ghetto will be murdered here. In total, about 800,000 people were gassed in Treblinka.

July 19: Heinrich Himmler, head of the SS, orders that all Polish Jews be deported to death camps by the end of the year.

July 23: Adam Czerniaków, chairman of the Warsaw Ghetto Jewish Council, is ordered by the Germans to arrange the deportation of 6,000 Jews a day. He commits suicide instead. By September 12, 265,000 Jews will be deported from the Warsaw ghetto.

1943

March: Himmler orders the extermination camps at Treblinka, Belzec, and Sobibor to be shut down.

July: The death camp at Belzec is the first to shut down.

August 2: Jewish prisoners, armed with stolen German pistols, rifles, and hand grenades, revolt at Treblinka and set the concentration camp on fire. Of the 350 to 400 prisoners who escape, only 100 elude recapture or execution.

August 19: The last victims are gassed at Treblinka.

October 14: An inmate revolt kills eleven SS guards and several Ukrainian guards at Sobibor. Of the 600 Jews who are incarcerated in the camp, 200 are killed during the revolt, 300 escape, and only 100 are recaptured.

November: The death camp at Treblinka is dismantled and shut down.

December: The death camp at Sobibor is dismantled and abandoned.

1944

June 6: The Allies invade Normandy, France.

July 23: The Russian army liberates the extermination camp in Majdanek, Poland, and finds about a thousand inmates still alive. The Nazis had been unable to complete the evacuation of the camp before the Red Army arrived.

August 2: The Gypsy camp at Auschwitz is exterminated; nearly three thousand Gypsies are murdered.

August 20: U.S. planes bomb the I.G. Farben chemical factory in Buna, five miles from the Auschwitz death camps. Later in the year, U.S. secretary of war John J. McCloy refuses requests from international groups to bomb

Auschwitz, claiming that doing so would hinder the war effort.

October 7: One of the four crematoriums at Auschwitz-Birkenau is blown up in a revolt by Jewish and Polish *sonderkommando*. During the fighting, 853 *sonderkommando* and 70 German SS officers are killed. The explosives had been smuggled in by women prisoners who are later executed by the Germans. About 600 prisoners escaped; approximately half are later found and shot.

1945

January–March: The SS orders that all prisoners in the remaining concentration camps in Poland be evacuated to camps in Austria and central Germany. These massive evacuations take place mostly on foot, and a high percentage of the marchers die along the way from starvation, exposure, exhaustion, or beatings by their guards. Those who cannot keep up are shot and left on the road.

January 17: The final roll call is taken at Auschwitz; the Nazis count 67,012 prisoners.

January 18: The advance of the Russians into Poland forces the Germans to evacuate the concentration camps at Auschwitz. Approximately sixty thousand prisoners are marched to concentration camps in Germany; more than fifteen thousand die during the march.

January 27: Russian troops liberate Auschwitz and find seven thousand inmates who are barely alive.

April: Units of the U.S. Army liberate Buchenwald, Dachau, and other concentration camps in Germany.

April 15: British and Canadian forces reach the Bergen-Belsen concentration camp and liberate the remaining prisoners. About twenty-eight thousand prisoners will die from starvation, illness, and injuries between April 15 and June 20.

April 30: Hitler commits suicide in Berlin.

May 8: Germany surrenders, ending the war in Europe.

August 8: Japan surrenders, ending the war in the Pacific region.

November 20: High-ranking Nazi officials and guards at concentration camps go on trial for war crimes in Nuremberg.

1946
October 1: The verdicts of the Nuremberg Trials are announced; nineteen defendants are found guilty and three are acquitted.

October 15: Convicted of war crimes during the Nuremberg Trials, Göring commits suicide with cyanide hours before his execution.

December 1946–April 1949: The Americans are in charge of the Subsequent Nuremberg Proceedings, a series of twelve trials of 185 Nazi doctors, industrialists, and military, government, and SS leaders, among others. Of the 142 defendants who were found guilty, only 25 received the death penalty, and 13 sentences were later commuted.

1947
April 16: Poland hangs former Auschwitz commandant Rudolf Höss at the Auschwitz concentration camp for his war crimes.

For Further Research

Lucie Adelsberger, *Auschwitz: A Doctor's Story*. Trans. Susan Ray. Boston: Northeastern University Press, 1995.

Jean Améry, *At the Mind's Limits: Contemplations by a Survivor on Auschwitz and Its Realities*. Trans. Sidney Rosenfeld and Stella P. Rosenfeld. New York: Schocken Books, 1986.

Eugène Aroneanu, ed., *Inside the Concentration Camps: Eyewitness Accounts of Life in Hitler's Death Camps*. Trans. Thomas Whissen. Westport, CT: Praeger, 1996.

Benjamin Bender, *Glimpses: Through Holocaust and Liberation*. Berkeley, CA: North Atlantic Books, 1995.

Michael Berenbaum, *The World Must Know: The History of the Holocaust as Told in the United States Holocaust Memorial Museum*. Boston: Little, Brown, 1993.

Sara Tuvel Bernstein, *The Seamstress: A Memoir of Survival*. New York: Putnam, 1997.

Livia Bitton-Jackson, *I Have Lived a Thousand Years: Growing Up in the Holocaust*. New York: Simon & Schuster Books for Young Readers, 1997.

Thomas Toivi Blatt, *From the Ashes of Sobibor: A Story of Survival*. Evanston, IL: Northwestern University Press, 1997.

Lucy S. Dawidowicz, ed., *A Holocaust Reader*. New York: Behrman House, 1976.

Jack Eisner, *The Survivor of the Holocaust*. New York: Kensington Books, 1995.

Leo Fettman, as told to Paul M. Howey, *Shoah: Journey from the Ashes: A Personal Story of Triumph over the Holocaust*. Omaha, NE: Six Points Press, 1999.

Viktor E. Frankl, *Man's Search for Meaning: An Introduction to Logotherapy.* Part 1. Trans. Ilse Lasch. 3rd ed. New York: Touchstone Press, 1984.

Hedi Fried, *The Road to Auschwitz: Fragments of a Life.* Ed. and trans. Michael Meyer. Lincoln: University of Nebraska Press, 1996.

Rena Kornreich Gelissen with Heather Dune Macadam, *Rena's Promise: A Story of Sisters in Auschwitz.* Boston: Beacon Press, 1995.

Martin Gilbert, *The Boys: The Untold Story of 732 Young Concentration Camp Survivors.* New York: Henry Holt, 1996.

Daniel Jonah Goldhagen, *Hitler's Willing Executioners: Ordinary Germans and the Holocaust.* New York: Vintage Books, 1997.

Joshua M. Greene and Shiva Kumar, eds., *Witness: Voices from the Holocaust.* New York: Free Press, 2000.

Adolf Hitler, *Mein Kampf.* Trans. Ralph Manhein. New York: Mariner Books, 1999.

The Holocaust Chronicle: A History in Words and Pictures. Lincolnwood, IL: Publications International, 2000.

Ernst Klee, Willi Dressen, and Volker Riess, eds., *"The Good Old Days": The Holocaust as Seen by Its Perpetrators and Bystanders.* Trans. Deborah Burnstone. New York: Konecky & Konecky, 1991.

Lucette Matalon Lagnado and Sheila Cohn Dekel, *Children of the Flames: Dr. Josef Mengele and the Untold Story of the Twins of Auschwitz.* New York: Penguin, 1991.

Claude Lanzmann, *Shoah: An Oral History of the Holocaust: The Complete Text of the Film.* New York: Pantheon, 1985.

Anita Lasker-Wallfisch, *Inherit the Truth: A Memoir of Survival and the Holocaust.* New York: Thomas Dunne Books, 2000.

Olga Lengyel, *Five Chimneys.* Chicago: Ziff-Davis, 1972.

Primo Levi, *Survival in Auschwitz: The Nazi Assault on Humanity.* Trans. Stuart Woolf. New York: Touchstone Press, 1996.

Rhoda G. Lewin, ed., *Witnesses to the Holocaust: An Oral History.* Boston: Twayne, 1990.

Jeremy Noakes and Geoffrey Pridham, *Foreign Policy, War, and Racial Extermination.* Vol. 3 of *Nazism, 1919–1945: A Documentary Reader.* Exeter, England: University of Exeter Press, 1988.

Sara Nomberg-Przytyk, *Auschwitz: True Tales from a Grotesque Land.* Ed. Eli Pfefferkorn and David H. Hirsch. Trans. Roslyn Hirsch. Chapel Hill: University of North Carolina Press, 1985.

Miklos Nyiszli, *Auschwitz: A Doctor's Eyewitness Account.* Trans. Tibère Kremer and Richard Seaver. New York: Arcade, 1993.

Helen Sendyk, *The End of Days.* New York: St. Martin's Press, 1992.

Eve Nussbaum Soumerai and Carol D. Schulz, *Daily Life During the Holocaust.* Westport, CT: Greenwood Press, 1998.

Steven Spielberg and Survivors of the Shoah Visual History Foundation, *The Last Days.* New York: St. Martin's Press, 1999.

Elie Wiesel, *Night; Dawn; Day.* Northvale, NJ: Jason Aronson, 1985.

Samuel Willenberg, *Surviving Treblinka.* Ed. Wladyslaw T. Bartoszewski. Trans. Naftali Greenwood. New York: Basil Blackwell, 1989.

Index